Best Career and Education Web Sites

A Quick Guide to Online Job Search

SIXTH EDITION

Anne Wolfinger

JIST Works
America's Career Publisher®

Best Career and Education Web Sites, Sixth Edition

© 2009 by JIST Publishing
Published by JIST Works, an imprint of JIST Publishing
7321 Shadeland Station, Suite 200
Indianapolis, IN 46256
Phone: 800-648-JIST   Fax: 800-454-7839   E-mail: info@jist.com

Visit our Web site at **www.jist.com** for information on JIST, free job search tips, book chapters, and ordering instructions for our many products!

See the back of this book for additional JIST titles and ordering information. Quantity discounts are available for JIST books. Have future editions of JIST books automatically delivered to you on publication through our convenient standing order program. Please call our Sales Department at 800-648-5478 for a free catalog and more information.

Trade Product Line Manager: Lori Cates Hand
Contributing Writer: Dave Anderson
Interior Designer: Debbie Berman
Cover Designers: Nick Anderson and Alan Evans
Page Layout: Toi Davis
Proofreaders: Linda Seifert and Paula Lowell
Indexer: Kelly D. Henthorne

Printed in the United States of America

14 13 12 11 10 09   9 8 7 6 5 4 3 2 1

Library of Congress Cataloging-in-Publication Data
Wolfinger, Anne.
    Best career and education Web sites : a quick guide to online job search / Anne Wolfinger. -- 6th ed.
        p. cm.
    Includes index.
    ISBN 978-1-59357-700-1 (alk. paper)
  1. Job hunting--Computer network resources. 2. Vocational guidance--Computer network resources. 3. Labor market--Computer network resources. 4. Internet. 5. World Wide Web. I. Title.
  HF5382.75.U6W65 2009
  025.06'331702--dc22
                     2008052307

We have been careful to provide accurate information in this book, but it is possible that errors and omissions have been introduced. Please consider this in making any career plans or other important decisions. Trust your own judgment above all else and in all things.

Trademarks: All brand names and product names used in this book are trade names, service marks, trademarks, or registered trademarks of their respective owners.

ISBN 978-1-59357-700-1

Contents

Career Exploration Information   67

Finding and Applying for Job Openings   95

Researching Employer and Labor Market Information   131

Military Careers   143

7   Self-Employment and Small Business   165

8   Temporary Work, Contract Employment, Freelancing, Teleworking, and Volunteering   185

Glossary   203

Index   213

About This Book

One of the biggest challenges we face as we enter the working world is to find or choose a career path that supports us financially, challenges us mentally, and helps us grow our unique talents. For many people, this is an ongoing challenge as we make career shifts either out of choice or necessity.

Best Career and Education Web Sites is designed to help you take advantage of the powerful resources of the Internet. You'll find the Web sites carefully selected and grouped to help you find the information you want. In most sections, you have a choice of Web sites to work with, so if you don't find what you want at one you can visit another. If you want to dig more deeply, we show you how as well.

Information is one piece of career decision-making, and an important one. But there's also you. You are a unique mix of abilities, interests, talents, imagination, dreams, and possibilities. You have a lot to contribute to your future, your family, your community, your profession, and the world in general. When you take charge of your career, you look first at who you are, figure out what questions to ask, look for information to help you, and filter out the rest.

So take charge, take heart, and let us help you along the way.

Best wishes,

Anne Wolfinger

Internet Tips and Electronic Resumes

The Internet has revolutionized how we find information. Career descriptions, college entrance requirements, financial aid facts, job openings in your hometown or across the world—it's all online. If you can find it.

Because the online world presents so many opportunities, it can be hard to figure out the best places to begin. That's why we've put together the very best career and education Web sites to let you use the Internet as a powerful tool in your career and education decisions. We've done the research for you by selecting and evaluating more than 350 sites.

Here's what we looked for. To be included in this book, sites have to offer quality information, the bulk of it free of charge. Sites primarily promoting fee-based services or products were, for the most part, excluded. Also, we like sites that explain what they are, usually with an "About us" link at the bottom of the page. Another biggie we looked for was a statement of the site's privacy policy, which is especially important if you provide any personal information (you'll read more about this in the sidebar "Protect Your Privacy"). Finally, we're not fond of ads, but cut the sites some slack if their content is good despite the distraction.

If you want to investigate further, we give you ideas for doing that, too. Not only do we talk about searching for additional career and education information online, we also point out when a Web site can lead you to further information and to other related sites, which many of them do.

Before we get started describing our sites, we'll tell you a little about finding and using information on the Internet, including tips for protecting your privacy. In addition, we cover the basics of how to create and use an electronic resume.

Realize first that "the Internet" is basically just a giant network of computers, all connected to allow people to communicate and to share and find information. The most common ways people use the Internet—and the ones we talk about in this book—include the following:

→ **The World Wide Web (WWW or the Web).** The Web lets you access information on Web sites, which can include text, pictures, video, audio, and more. Most of the Internet resources discussed in this book are Web sites.

→ **Electronic mail (e-mail).** E-mail lets you send written messages to friends, relatives, and potential employers and lets them easily reply to you. Your messages can make it across the building or across the ocean within minutes or even seconds. You can also send your resume and apply for jobs via e-mail. We'll talk more about that in the section "Using Electronic Resumes."

→ **Blogs (Web logs).** A blog is a Web site where entries are regularly posted, journal-style, and shared with readers. Although blogs tend to be more personal in nature, there is value to blogging when it comes to your career. Blogging can lead to networking opportunities and unearth potential job leads.

The World Wide Web

The World Wide Web is most often accessed through a piece of software called a *Web browser,* usually Internet Explorer. (If you use an online service such as AOL, you also have the option of using its built-in Web browser.) Each lets you navigate the Web through a graphical user interface, using the mouse to point and click your way to the information you need.

The point-and-click nature of the Web works because of the use of *hypertext.* Hypertext documents on the Web contain *hyperlinks* (or *links*), which connect you to other related information. When you click a word, phrase, button, or image that contains a link, a new Web page comes up on the screen. You can then choose to continue along that line of information, go back to your original location, or go off in yet another direction.

How Fast Is Fast Enough?

It's important for you to tap into the Internet to make the most of your job search. But how to tap in? Do you need a broadband connection to get the most out of your Web surfing experience? Is cable really better than DSL? Is there a way to access the power of the Internet without paying 30 or 40 dollars a month? There are currently three ways to access the Internet: through a cable modem (and a high-speed Internet service provider), DSL (digital subscriber line), or a dialup connection through your phone line. Each of these options varies in speed and price (with cable being the fastest and most costly).

The truth is, you can send and receive e-mail using almost any kind of Internet access. The faster speeds provided by cable and DSL connections help when downloading or uploading files or visiting highly interactive or graphically intricate Web sites. Still, don't feel like you have to pay $50 a month for the fastest download speed. Instead, visit your local library and take advantage of its free high-speed connections when you have serious work to do online.

Understanding Web Addresses

Web addresses (called *URLs,* or *Uniform Resource Locators*) point you to specific Web sites on the Internet. A Web address works just like a postal address, identifying where on the Internet that particular Web site "lives." Although these addresses at first look somewhat confusing, there is a logic to them. Let's take apart the address http://www.jist.com/books.shtm and examine it piece by piece to see how it is put together.

domain name

```
http://www.jist.com/books.shtm
```

protocol   file name

The beginning of any Internet address is the *protocol,* which tells the computer which part of the Internet you're using. For Web sites, you almost always see **http://**, which stands for Hypertext Transfer Protocol. Luckily, you don't need to type this part of the URL into a newer Web browser—it just assumes it's there.

www, which stands for *World Wide Web,* is often part of a Web address. Sometimes people leave it off when they talk about Web addresses (saying "jist. com" instead of "www.jist.com," for example). Just be aware that some URLs do not contain the www. For those sites, we've included the full URL with **http://** (such as http://mapping-your-future.org) so that you won't add the www and get lost. Also, variations are starting to pop up, such as "www2." Just type the Web address exactly as it appears in the book, and you will be fine.

jist.com is the *domain name.* It's basically the most important part of the Internet address; it gets you to the company, organization, or other entity that owns that domain. The part before the dot often is similar to the name of the company or other entity that owns the Web site. (In this case, "jist" stands for JIST Publishing.) The letters after the dot (the *extension*) identify what type of organization it is. Most U.S. Web sites prefer to use .com, .org, and .edu. Here are the most common extensions:

.com for a commercial site

.biz for companies

.edu for a university or educational institution

.gov for a government agency

.net for a network

.org for an association or organization

.mil for a branch of the U.S. Military

.info for an informational site

.name for individuals

books.shtm is the file name of the information you're viewing—the name of that file on the computer you are visiting on the Internet. The last part of the file name is usually htm, html, or shtml. (Sometimes you see newer file names that end in .asp or another group of letters, but just type them in exactly as you see them.) *htm* and *html* mean *Hypertext Markup Language,* the language of the Web; an *shtml* file is just an html file that uses a slightly different technology. As with word-processing or spreadsheet files, you can copy, print, or save an htm, html, or shtml file.

Those are the basics of Web addresses. Of course, they can be much longer than our example because of the complexity of content on a Web site. You often see directory paths between the domain name and file name, located between slashes. Directory paths just tell the host computer where to look for the file you want. A Web address can also specify a location within a file (a section farther down the page, for example) or show the results of search criteria you've entered.

The Power of Portals

Some people like to set a favorite search engine as their browser's home page so that they can quickly start looking for the information they need every time they go online. Many search engines and directories have transformed into portals that let you view your local news, weather, e-mail, and more on the same page you search from. Therefore, using one as your home page can be handy (and simple to set up—most search engines help you do it in one or two clicks).

Search-engine portals can be powerful, time-saving tools in your job search. From a single Web site, they allow you to do the following:

- Get a free e-mail address. You can use this address just for your job search, to keep your personal and business correspondence separate.
- Locate employer contact information through links to online white pages and yellow pages.
- Find your way to an interview. Use the mapping feature on some portal pages (such as Yahoo!) to map the route from your house to the interview, and then print it for take-along convenience.
- Stay informed. You can personalize your portal and have it deliver news, stock reports, and more based on the demographic data and preferences you provide when you register.
- Prepare for the inevitable job interview small talk by reading late-breaking headlines right on your search-engine page.
- Figure out how to dress for tomorrow's interview (and how much time to allow to get there) by checking the local weather forecast.

Searching the Web

Search engines and directories are special Web sites that have indexed large portions of the Internet. They allow you to specify the information you are looking for, and then they bring up a list of Web sites, or pages from Web sites, that meet your criteria. Although Web browsers such as Internet Explorer include a Search option on their toolbars, there are many other ways to search. We'll talk about some of the options next.

But first, let's look at the basics of successful Internet searching:

1. Pick your topic. The first step is to identify what you want to research and to define it as specifically as possible.

2. Pick your search engine. Different search engines can be better for different types of topics, or for broader as opposed to very specific searches, so your topic can influence which search engine you use. In the next sections we'll talk more about different types of search engines and directories and when to use each.

3. Type in two or three words, or *keywords,* to tell the search engine what you're looking for.

Boolean Logic

Many search engines use Boolean logic, named after nineteenth-century mathematician George Boole, who invented it. Boolean logic uses the terms AND and OR. An AND search means that the search engine will turn up only the results that contain both items or terms you have listed. An OR search means you'll settle for either one. Nine times out of ten, an OR search gives you a bigger list.

For example, I did a simple search on Google for librarian AND salaries and got 994,000 results. Searching for librarian OR salaries produced 95,100,000 results. My best search results resulted from typing in "librarian salaries" with quotation marks, which tells Google to look for that specific phrase. This search returned 25,300 results, many of which looked promising.

Search engines may simplify matters for you. Look for an "advanced search" link or button, which usually produces a list of search choices for you, like all the words, the exact phrase, any of the words, or none of the words. Other options may include language, date, or domain type.

Consider investing a little time in becoming an expert searcher by checking out some online tutorials. See the section "More Search Options" for some places to start.

The two main varieties of search engines are Internet directories and indexed search engines. Some, however, combine both types on the same site for extra searching power, and others have morphed themselves into multifeatured personalized portal sites. (See the earlier sidebar "The Power of Portals.")

When deciding which type of search engine to use, consider what you're looking for. Directories are handy for exploring a general concept or broad, open-ended questions. Browsing through a list of categories might alert you to related topics you hadn't previously considered. Indexed search engines are best for a more narrowly defined topic.

Internet Directories

Internet directories organize Web sites into categories that let visitors drill down from broad to very specific topics. For example, let's say you wanted to use Yahoo!, the best-known Internet directory, to get a list of sites that provide information on the federal minimum-wage law. You could drill down through the categories as follows: Business and Economy: Employment and Work: Employment and Workplace Issues: Minimum Wage. Directories usually aim to provide just the "best" sites in each category, rather than creating a comprehensive index of as many Web sites as possible.

Many Internet directories also give you the option of doing a keyword search, but beware: They might be searching just their own directories and not the entire Web. Or, if they do include the rest of the Web in their search, their directory sites might get top billing over other Web sites. How do you know? Sometimes they tell you, but for the behind-the-scenes story, visit the Search Engine Showdown Web site at www.notess.com/search/, which is described in the section "Further Search Help."

Here are a couple examples of Internet directories:

Open Directory Project
http://dmoz.org

> The AOL-administered Open Directory Project (ODP), the largest human-edited Web directory, is maintained entirely by volunteer editors around the world. Editors are responsible for selecting, organizing, updating, and annotating the links in their own categories. (Are you an expert on a subject? Consider signing up to help!) Unlike some other directories, ODP never charges to list URLs. On the downside, the quality of different categories can be inconsistent. Several major search engines use ODP data to power their own directories.

Yahoo!

www.yahoo.com

> Search or drill down through the Yahoo! categories, or personalize your own Yahoo! home page to include access to e-mail, an appointment calendar, local weather, headline news, and more. Click Help for search tips and other information on using and personalizing the site. With a simple click or two, you can also make Yahoo! your home page.

Those Annoying Ads

Okay, we admit it. We don't like ads. However, they are a fact of life on the Internet, especially for Web sites that rely on advertising to support their content and services. Ads range from the rather unobtrusive Google text ads to pop-ups, pop-unders, and, the most distracting, action ads. Web technology can track your linking activity, and sophisticated Web sites can tailor the information, especially the advertising, you see based on it.

Here are some suggestions to help you keep your ad exposure under control:

- You can choose whether to use ad-laden sites. Chances are excellent that you can find another site with the information or services you're looking for. We refuse to use sites with **pop-under ads,** which appear after you exit the site.
- **Pop-up blockers,** as their name implies, can prevent pop-up ads that appear on some sites and force you to click through them to get to what you really want. If you download the Yahoo! toolbar, for example, you also get a pop-up blocker.
- **Ad-aware software** detects and removes behavior-tracking spyware, data mining, aggressive advertising tactics, and tracking components. A personal version is available free of charge from www.lavasoft.com.

Indexed Search Engines

Indexed search engines vary in what they cover and how they categorize sites, but each uses computerized indexing rather than humans to index Web sites and then allows visitors to search through that index for information of interest.

To understand why you receive different results from each search engine, realize that some search engines index the entire contents of a Web page. Others index only specific parts, such as the title or top heading, or hone in on keywords that the Web page author embeds at the top of the page (inside a *metatag*) to describe that page's content. For example, some of the keywords for jist.com are resumes, job search, career, jobs, books, videos, reference, workbooks, assessments, and cover letters. Each applies to the types of material JIST publishes.

Each search engine also uses different criteria to rank Web sites, so one of the top sites to show up in one search engine might appear far down the list—or not at all—in another. These rankings can depend on how often your keyword appears on a particular Web page, how popular that page is (for example, how often it is linked to from other Web sites), or a number of other factors, including advertising. "Sponsor" sites pay fees to appear at the top of search lists.

Keyword searches are common, and you'll find them not only in search engines, but also within many Web sites. Many of the job banks described in chapter 4, for example, offer a keyword search to help you sort through their job listings.

Not only do search engines index the Internet differently, but each displays your results in different ways. Some, for example, show you the total number of pages found. Others display just the titles of the pages. Still others provide annotations from their partner directory or descriptions provided by the Web page creators themselves.

As mentioned in the sidebar "Boolean Logic," many search engines offer you the choice of doing simple or advanced searches. Advanced searching usually gives you more control. A good plan is to try a simple search first and see what happens and then switch to an advanced search if you are unhappy with your initial results.

Here are some examples of indexed search engines:

Google

www.google.com

Google's sense of humor is apparent in its penchant for decorating its logo to celebrate holidays and special occasions. Your search terms are highlighted within the results in an excerpt from that page, and sponsored links are clearly marked at the top and sides of results lists. Google also offers special searches for news, different file types, and a large number of advanced search options. Google offers a downloadable toolbar for Internet Explorer so that you can do an instant Google search at any time without first going to the Google home page. You also can make Google your home page in a click or two. You can personalize your Google site and use any number of other Google services, including news alerts, blogging and blog searches, full-text book searches, mailing lists and discussion groups, and Google's version of e-mail (less-than-creatively called g-mail).

Ask.com

www.ask.com

> Download the Ask.com toolbar to quickly access Ask.com's powerful search engine, do a quick word lookup in the dictionary, or e-mail any Web page to a friend. Ask.com uses a unique search function that locates communities on the Web within their specific subject areas, producing search results that come with suggestions for narrowing or expanding your search. You can even install a desktop version of Ask.com to index the contents of your own computer, giving you high tech searching power closer to home—a big plus if you can't remember the file name or folder for your electronic resume.

Live Search

www.live.com

> Live Search is software giant Microsoft's search engine, accessible through the address above and through MSN.com's web portal. You can use the standard search, or try one of the more focused search engines, including ones for images, classifieds, books, maps, videos, academic information, and more. One added bonus: you can sign up with Live Search to receive a cash-back bonus on items purchased over the Internet. It pays to shop online.

More Search Options

Your other choices here usually allow you to go bigger (with metasearch engines that search a number of search engine databases at once) or smaller (with subject-specific or specialized databases). Metasearch engines can save time by searching a number of places at once, but it's harder to do an advanced search, because you don't have access to each site's tools. Smaller or subject-specific databases can let you do a more focused search when you need a very specific piece of information, such as a phone number. The Web has hundreds of search engines. To find more, try exploring the sites listed in the next section, or check out the Internet Search Engine database at www.isedb.com.

Dogpile

www.dogpile.com

> Dogpile has "all the best search engines piled into one," including Google, Yahoo!, MSN, and Ask. Its front page offers options to search for Web pages, images, audio or video files, news, yellow pages (for companies), and white pages (for individuals). Search results indicate where the sites were found. Sponsored sites are clearly indicated. Advanced search options offer you more searching power. Download the Dogpile toolbar for quick desktop access.

Clusty

http://clusty.com

> Another metasearch engine, Clusty searches a number of search engines and provides results both in a typical top-results list and in "clusters" of information. Clusters group results into several related subjects; you can choose any cluster to see the actual sites found. Each result shows the search engine(s) it came from, and you can click the preview icon to see a snippet of the site without having to load the whole page and move away from your results list.

WhitePages.com

www.whitepages.com

> At WhitePages.com, you can find a person, a phone number, an area code, a ZIP code, a toll-free number, maps, and more. It's an all-around useful site. You can also do reverse lookups, in which you enter a phone number and get an address. This can come in handy for those "blind" job ads.

Further Search Help

Search Engine Showdown

www.notess.com/search/

> Librarian Greg Notess provides this "users' guide to Web searching" to help you make the most out of your Internet searches. You'll find reviews of search engines, news, statistics, tutorials, feature comparisons, and

more. Search Engine Showdown also compares and discusses the major Internet directories, news and phone number search engines, and other related sites. It's the place to start for information on all the major search engines.

The Spider's Apprentice

www.monash.com/spidap.html

The Spider's Apprentice is "a helpful guide to Web search engines." Want to know how your favorite stacks up against the competition? In addition to answers to frequently asked questions and helpful search strategies, The Spider's Apprentice conducts in-depth analysis and rankings.

Web Search Strategies

www.learnwebskills.com/search/main.html

For a straightforward tutorial on honing your Web searching skills, try Web Search Strategies from Internet training pro Debbie Flanagan. Complete with exercises, Web Search Strategies guides you step-by-step through the seemingly complicated world of search engines. You'll learn about using search engines, subject directories, metasearch engines, and specialty databases. It includes in-depth instruction on searching the most popular search engines, as well as practice searches to get you started.

RSS Feeds and Readers

Imagine your computer telling *you* when a new job has been posted that you might be interested in, rather than you having to search for that information yourself? Or getting the latest headlines from a dozen different online news sources delivered directly to your desktop, all in one easy-to-read format? RSS makes this possible.

RSS stands for Rich Site Summary (or Really Simple Syndication) and is a relatively recent innovation in how we access and deliver information. RSS allows Internet sites—from news sites to blogs to job boards—to deliver the latest content directly to a designated location (known as an RSS reader or aggregator). RSS helps you stay informed by pulling the most current information from sites you're interested in without you having to visit the sites themselves. You simply subscribe to the RSS feed on the sites you visit often (provided they have a feed to subscribe to) and then use your RSS reader to retrieve all the new content. The reader notifies you when new content is available, saving you time. Plus, all of your feeds come to the same place—your desktop, your home page, your cell phone, your iPod—making it easier than ever to keep up with the latest career news, advice, and opportunities.

The number of Web sites with RSS capabilities increases by the minute. You can subscribe to RSS feeds at Monster, CareerBuilder, the *Wall Street Journal,* and Google News. Many of the Internet's most popular and valuable blogs offer RSS feeds. Individual companies you might be interested in working for might have an RSS feed informing you of the latest company news and possible job opportunities.

Of course, in order to start subscribing to RSS feeds, you'll need to download an RSS reader—the simple program that displays the contents of the feed in an organized, easily readable format. Two popular readers include Google Reader (www.google.com/reader) and Feed Demon (www.newsgator.com/Individuals/FeedDemon/). Many companies that offer readers for desktops also offer them for mobile phones and other portable electronic devices as well.

The average student or job seeker doesn't always have an hour every day to hit all of their favorite Web sites and see if anything has changed. If that describes you as well, you should check out your favorite sites (and many of the ones listed in this book) and see whether they offer RSS subscriptions. Then download a reader and start saving time.

E-mail

Electronic mail (e-mail) is the Internet's most popular feature—and for good reason. E-mail lets you stay in touch with everyone from friends to co-workers, sending messages nearly instantly within the office, across the street, or around the world.

E-mail is the most basic tool in your Internet job search. It's nearly impossible today to conduct an effective job search without e-mail, and it's impossible to do an effective Internet job search without having a handle on e-mail basics.

E-mail is important because it

 Allows employers to contact you quickly and easily

 Allows you to send your electronic resume to potential employers

➡ Allows you to receive notifications from personal job search agents (for more on job search agents, see chapter 4)

➡ Allows employers to see you as a technologically savvy applicant

➡ Allows you to network online with others in your field

E-mail software comes bundled with computer operating systems (such as Outlook in Windows) as well as in the software for online services such as America Online (AOL). You'll need an account from an Internet Service Provider (ISP) to use the e-mail software that comes with your computer or to use other free or commercial e-mail software you buy or download. (Two popular free e-mail programs are Eudora, available at www.eudora.com, and Pegasus Mail, available at www.pmail.com.) You need information from your ISP to set up your e-mail software initially, but most walk you through the process over the phone in just a couple minutes. You can also sign up for free Web-based e-mail service on a number of Internet sites.

Protect Your Privacy

Any time you register at a Web site, download a toolbar or free software, subscribe to a free e-newsletter, buy a product online, or post your resume, you expose yourself to a potential loss of some of your privacy. When you use the Internet, information is being gathered about you whether or not you know it (see the preceding sidebar, "Those Annoying Ads").

Get smart about your privacy. Here are some suggestions:

- Look for a statement of a Web site's privacy policy, and read it. In particular, look for information on who the site shares user data with. If you can opt out of information sharing, do so.

- Be careful each time you are asked for personal information on a Web site. Complete only the required information, and, depending on the site, even consider fudging on the truth.

- Be selective as to the number of sites you register with. The more times you provide your name, e-mail address, and other information, the greater your exposure to spam and unwanted junk mail.

- Never respond to an e-mail asking you to "update" your personal information, especially financial info. Phishing is an Internet scam that attempts to collect private user information to be used for identity theft. You receive an e-mail directing you to an authentic-looking Web site, where you are asked to update personal information, such as passwords and credit card, Social Security, and bank account numbers. A legitimate Web site or organization would already have these.

- Control your cookies. A cookie is a text-only string that gets entered into your browser's memory. Cookies allow Web sites to personalize information, help with online sales or service, or collect demographic information. You can find out more about cookies and how to set your browser to control them at Cookie Central, www.cookiecentral.com/faq/.

- Use free e-mail to be ultra-selective about who you give your "main" e-mail address to, or use a free address temporarily as a place to receive job notices.

E-mail Addresses

E-mail addresses, like Web site addresses, provide a standard way to locate someone on the Internet. They are put together in a fairly straightforward manner that makes sense when you understand what each part of the e-mail address does. Let's take a typical e-mail address and look at each part of it:

info@jist.com

The first part of an e-mail address (**info**) is the user name, which identifies a unique mailbox. You can usually pick your own user name, but on big Web-based e-mail providers, or online services such as AOL, so many people are using e-mail that you might have to add numbers or letters to make your user name unique. (This is how people end up with e-mail addresses with user names like "joezzz" and "fred123.")

Every e-mail address includes the **@** symbol. This is how you know it is an e-mail address rather than a Web site or another Internet address.

The part after the @ sign is the domain name (**jist.com**). Just like the domain portion of a Web site address, this lets you know the company or organization that the e-mail address is part of.

Signature, Please!

Your e-mail *signature* is simply a little block of text that is automatically included at the bottom of each of your outgoing e-mail messages. It can include your name and contact information, a quote, a pitch, a tagline, or a message that sums up you and your qualifications.

Almost all e-mail software and Web-based e-mail allow you to create a signature. Why not make yours useful to employers and show your enthusiasm? A job seeker might try something like this on outgoing cover letters:

Looking forward to putting my five years of (specific work experience) to work for you.

Or:

Member, (name of job-related professional associations to which you belong)

Put your contact information in your signature to make sure you don't forget to include it in the e-mail cover letters you send. Get creative if you want. Test it. But be sure to keep your signature brief and professional. Don't impose on readers by including huge quotes that are longer than your e-mail message itself, for example.

Free Web-Based E-mail

In addition to free e-mail software packages such as Eudora and Pegasus mail, a number of companies and Web sites offer free Web-based e-mail service.

So what's in it for them? These Internet companies provide you free e-mail in return for your demographic information, which is valuable to them and their advertisers. You get the service for free, but you have to look at ads every time you use your online e-mail box. Some even e-mail you advertising in addition to the banner ads and other advertisements you see on the Web pages you use to access your e-mail. Check the site's privacy policy and opt out of such advertising if you can.

So what's in it for you? Web-based e-mail services allow you to read and send e-mail from any Internet-connected computer—at the library, at home, at work, at school, or at a friend's house. They also provide you with a consistent e-mail address: Even if you change ISPs and lose your e-mail address with your provider, your Web-based address stays the same. If you share an Internet account with others in your family, you can use Web-based e-mail to set up a private e-mail address. Some of these e-mail providers also include calendars and other add-ons to make Web-based e-mail even more useful.

You can use the Free E-mail Providers Guide at www.fepg.net to locate the Web mail that is right for you, or check out the following three free Web-based e-mail providers:

MSN Hotmail

www.hotmail.com

> In addition to a generous 5 GB of e-mail in-box storage, MSN Hotmail offers powerful spam filters and enhanced virus scanning and cleaning—important tools for keeping your computer healthy. MSN Hotmail is now part of the Windows Live family of services, which includes messaging, blog publishing, password-protected online file storage, and more—all free. To sign up for the whole shebang, go to http://get.live.com/.

Yahoo! Mail

http://mail.yahoo.com

> Yahoo! Mail scores high marks for its sophisticated security features, a configurable spam filter, and anti-virus scanning and cleaning. Yahoo! Mail was the first Web-based mail service to include a detailed address book, calendar, and notepad, and these work as well as ever. It also provides an online chat function so that you can instant message friends and keep in touch with people in your network. Yahoo! Mail is part of Yahoo!'s portal services.

Gmail

http://mail.google.com

> With powerful spam filters, optimal storage, and built in chat features, Google's version of e-mail offers many of the same advantages of the other popular e-mail services and is considered by many to have the easiest-to-use interface.

E-mail Savvy

During your job search, you've probably spent a lot of time developing your network of contacts. Why spend time scrolling through hundreds of old e-mail messages trying to find someone's contact information or messages on a specific topic? Use the capabilities of your e-mail software or Web mail to get organized.

(continued)

(continued)

Common e-mail functions include

- Setting up mailboxes (or folders) to archive and organize old messages
- Saving and organizing e-mail addresses in an address book
- Saving the e-mail addresses of a group of people together, which helps you send a message to the group without having to type each individual address
- Sorting e-mails by status, priority, sender, date, subject, and so on
- Setting up filters to automatically direct incoming mail to a particular folder or mailbox
- Setting up filters to automatically open, copy, print, or delete a message

Taking a moment to read your program's manual or Help menu can save you time and help you organize your all-important e-mail. Now that's a win-win proposition!

Using Electronic Resumes

Today, creating an electronic resume is almost the same as creating a regular resume. You just need to create and save your resume in Microsoft Word or similar word-processing software and take a couple of steps to change it into other commonly requested formats. You're then ready to post it online or e-mail it directly to employers.

Note: If you need help creating a resume, check out Susan Britton Whitcomb's *Résumé Magic*, or see the resume Web sites listed in chapter 4.

Types of Electronic Resumes

There are three common types of electronic resumes. This section explains how to create and when to use each.

 Microsoft Word. You'll often see job ads requesting that candidates send their resume in "Word format." They are asking for a copy of the file you create when you type up and save your resume in Microsoft Word. If you use another word-processing program to create your resume, such as WordPerfect, don't worry. You can save most documents in Microsoft

Word format. (Typically, all you have to do when saving your file is choose Save As from the File menu. Then select Microsoft Word from the options listed.)

→ **ASCII (or "plain-text") resumes.** ASCII resumes are the lowest common denominator of electronic resumes. Although they might look plain and boring, some employers prefer to receive this type of resume to help them scan more easily for keywords (see the next section) and to reduce their risk of catching a computer virus from Word resumes. The easiest way to create an ASCII resume is to open your Microsoft Word resume and select Save As from the File menu. In the "Save as type" list, select Plain Text, and click Save. (Ignore any warnings Word gives you about losing formatting.)

Your resume is then saved as plain text. You can check by looking in the directory where you saved it. Your original resume will be listed as *resumename*.doc, and your text resume will be listed as *resumename*.txt.

Open your plain-text resume in a program such as Windows Notepad. Just double-click the name of the .txt file when you are looking at your directory. Notice that all the special formatting from your Word resume, such as bold, underline, and bullets, has been lost. You need to go through your text resume in Notepad and make it look as nice as possible without using any special formatting, because this is exactly how an employer will see your resume. When you're done, just resave it.

→ **HTML (or "Web page") resumes.** You can put your resume online in the form of a Web page. This allows you to do things such as include links from your resume to projects you have done, your e-mail address, and other useful information for employers. Putting your resume online as a Web page also allows employers to find you. This is easier than ever before because of user-friendly graphical Web page editing software such as Microsoft FrontPage and free Web hosting services such as Tripod (www.tripod.lycos.com). You can even use Microsoft Word to create a basic HTML resume by choosing Save As from the File menu and then choosing Web Page from the "Save as type" list. Also, ask whether your school allows students to post resumes online, which might help employers find you from your school's Web site.

One of the things to be especially careful about with your Web page resume is to keep it looking as professional as possible. Because it is so easy to add pictures, music, and so on to a Web page, sometimes people go overboard and make employers look at family photos and listen to songs. You don't want to distract anyone looking at your HTML resume from its main point: you and your qualifications.

Using Keywords

You will want to use *keywords* to make your resume match the terms used in employers' job ads as closely as possible. These kinds of keywords are different from those discussed earlier with search engines. Keywords in this sense are the "hot" words (usually nouns) that are associated with a specific industry, profession, or job function. Using keywords is especially important if you are applying to large companies, which might use a computer to search through all the resumes they receive and reject any that don't have the right keywords. The best way around this is to be sure to include keywords to get your resume past the first cut.

Luckily, you've already put your resume in electronic format. This makes it easy for you to make changes and use the precise keyword terms mentioned in the ads.

Always be as specific as possible. Read each job ad carefully, and be ready and willing to make changes to your resume when applying for different positions.

Getting Your Resume Online

There are a couple of different ways to get your resume online and in front of employers. The first (and easier) way is to respond to employers who ask for a copy of your Microsoft Word or plain-text resume via e-mail. (If you don't have an e-mail address yet, check out the section "Free Web-Based E-mail" for ideas on how to get a free one.)

Employers who want a Word resume will want it as an e-mail attachment. Any e-mail software program lets you attach a file to a message. Just write a message including your cover letter, and then select the option in your software or in your Web mail to attach a file. Browse to the place you have saved your resume, and select that file to attach to your e-mail message. It will be sent with the message so that the employer can open it and see it just as you saved it.

Employers who specify a plain-text resume will want it either as an attachment or inside the e-mail message itself. If they want it inside the message, first type your cover letter as an e-mail to the employer. Then open your plain-text resume in Notepad and use copy and paste to include the text of your resume right under your cover letter.

The next way to get your resume online is to post it in a resume bank on one of the major job boards, such as Monster. (You'll find information on a bunch of these in chapter 4.) When you see the option to post your resume online, you usually get a form to fill out. Again, use copy and paste to transfer information from your resume into this form.

Using your resume electronically saves you and employers time, lets you tailor each resume for the specific job opening, and shows potential employers that you have some computer know-how. Many of the Web sites in this book give you the opportunity to use your electronic resume, so have it ready to go.

Career Portfolios

A portfolio is a collection of records that document your work experience, educational background, and the successes you've had in your career. It reflects your goals and values and demonstrates your skills and knowledge by displaying supporting documents and valuable information that won't be found on a resume. Such documents might include awards, certificates, diplomas, transcripts, and evaluations, as well as mission statements and letters of recommendation. Whenever feasible, samples of one's work make an excellent addition to the portfolio and can give employers a better idea of what you are capable of.

While portfolios have been around for centuries, their value has been limited save for those in professions that require them (artists and teachers, for example). But technological innovations of the past decade have changed all of that. The Internet—and several powerful tools that can be found online—have made it easier than ever for any job seeker to put together a portfolio that showcases their talents and to post it online for all the world to see. Such online portfolios are potent career tools as they provide job seekers with the potential to create a multimedia, multidimensional presentation—the kind of pitch that a one-page resume simply can't make.

While they are becoming more and more common, digital portfolios still aren't the document of choice for most job seekers (it will take some time before they replace the resume). However that only means that having a digital portfolio can help you to stand apart from the crowd. For more information on creating, storing, and sending digital portfolios online, see the section on career portfolios in chapter 4.

Blogs

Blogs, which is short for *Web logs*, are a relatively new addition to the online world. The idea of a blog is like an online journal or column, in which the writer posts short installments on a daily or weekly basis. Blogs can be all about personal things, or they can be more professional and focus on everything to do with a particular topic. It is these professional blogs that are most relevant to your career, job search, and education quest.

The importance of blogs to your career is twofold:

→ **Source of information:** First, they can be a timely, detailed, and more personal way to get career advice. The people who write blogs can be considered experts on their particular subjects (or at least they are very enthusiastic about them). You can use blogs to find out about job openings, what day-to-day life is like in a particular career, or what the very latest happenings are in the job market or a particular industry.

→ **Showcase of your talents:** If you can write a focused and professional blog related to your target career, it can actually help you land a job. Your blog will be one of the first things that comes up if an employer decides to search the Web for information about you. And it can demonstrate your interest and knowledge in your career field.

We have included the addresses of many relevant blogs among the listings of helpful sites in this book. To find blogs that are related to your career, see Google Blogsearch (www.google.com/blogsearch). To learn more about the art of blogging, see ProBlogger (www.problogger.net/).

CHAPTER 1

College and Financial Aid Information

We place great value on higher education—and with good reason. Higher education can bring a number of benefits, from career satisfaction to personal enhancement. It can dramatically increase the number and kinds of careers one is qualified for. However, the advantage that stands out the most is increased earning potential.

Take a look at these numbers. The U.S. Census Bureau reported in 2004 that the average wage for a college graduate working full-time was $51,206, or $23,291 more than high school grads—a million dollars more over the course of a 43-year career.

The lifelong increased earning potential for college graduates is a persuasive argument for a college education, but getting into and through college can be a job in itself. Fortunately, a number of Web sites can help you get started with planning for college, choosing a school, and funding your education. An investigation of them will save you or someone you love (and support) time and trouble as you begin your adventures in higher education.

Researching Colleges

These Web sites are the best places to begin looking for school-specific information. Most of them use a search tool to help you find what you're looking for. The number and types of schools they cover vary from site to site, as the descriptions show, so if you don't find what you're looking for at one, try another. Several also include information on financial aid, getting into schools, and much more, so spend some time browsing to see what is available.

BrainTrack
www.braintrack.com

> If you're interested in schools with an international flavor, you might check out BrainTrack—the Internet's most complete index of colleges, universities, and trade schools. You can use the search engine, or pick your continent (yes, it's that big), and narrow down by location from there. The end result is simply a collection of links to schools that might interest you, but if you have ever considered going to college in Iceland or Tanzania, this is a good place to start looking. Of course, they also have a directory of 7,000 U.S. schools that you can browse alphabetically or by state.

CampusTours.com
www.campustours.com

> "Virtual" college tours here range from straightforward online videos about a school to 360-degree panoramic images. Extras include maps, photos, webcams, and links to university Web sites. To take full advantage of CampusTours, make sure you have the latest versions of the QuickTime, Flash, Windows Media Player, RealPlayer, and IPIX plugins—all of which can be downloaded and installed from this site. Take the opportunity to view what each campus has to offer without having to travel.

College Navigator
http://nces.ed.gov/collegenavigator/

> Created by the U.S. Department of Education's National Center for Education Statistics, this handy tool will let you find colleges and programs based on several search options ranging from location and campus setting to cost, test scores, and even athletic teams and religious affiliations. There is no cost to use this program.

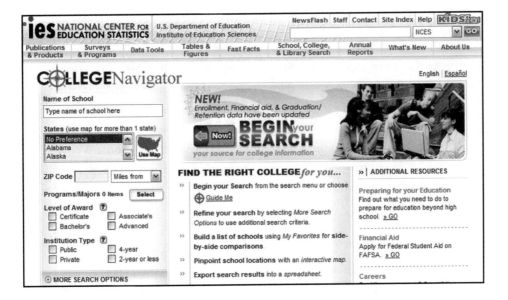

College Degree.com

www.collegedegree.com

> Sometimes all it takes to get a college degree is a computer, an Internet connection, lots of determination, and evenings off. Online or distance learning is one of the fastest-growing sectors in higher education, and College Degree.com can help you find an accredited, online program from the 115 colleges in its database. Use the Quick Degree Finder if you already have a pretty good idea what you are looking for, or you can browse by college, degree, or program. You can also use this site to search for scholarships by state and check out the library for articles on applying for and succeeding in an online degree program.

Community College Review

www.communitycollegereview.com

> Community College Review provides free, detailed profiles of community colleges across the U.S. The profiles include key statistics and demographic information; notes on each school's history, mission, and academics; and a form that you can use to get admissions information mailed or e-mailed to you. Colleges are initially searchable by state, although you can use your ZIP code to find the schools nearest you.

GradSchools.com

www.gradschools.com

> As the name implies, GradSchools.com lists only graduate school programs, but there are more than 60,000 of them. Select from a lengthy alphabetical list of programs, or choose your preferred part of the country. Online graduate programs are also listed. Your search results show the degrees each institution offers, with contact information and a Web link for more information. You can also register for free to save the results of your searches and learn even more about programs you are interested in.

myFootpath.com

www.myfootpath.com/Colleges.php

> The folks at myFootpath.com call themselves "experts in college admissions," and you'll find a lot of information on the process here. Read insightful articles on college admission, college preparation, and college life; search for specific schools and programs of interest; and research the best ways to fund your college education. If you have a particular school in mind, you can also purchase inside admissions reports on specific colleges to get in-depth information on the application process.

Petersons.com

www.petersons.com

> Peterson's is best known for its test-preparation and admissions guides, but it provides a generous amount of free information on this extensive site. Search for colleges, nursing programs, culinary schools, visual and performing arts schools, and more. Get contact information and find ways to apply online, or visit the schools' own sites for further information. If you're just beginning the college application process, Peterson's can help you get organized with its My Peterson's planning tool. By registering, you will be able to keep up with deadlines, practice for important entrance exams, get help with applications, download podcasts, and more.

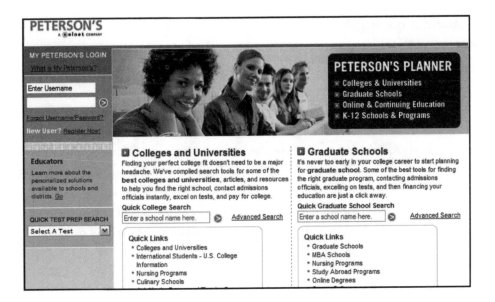

The Princeton Review

www.princetonreview.com

Search the Princeton Review's Web site database for colleges, business schools, law schools, medical schools, graduate schools, or graduate programs. If you're uncertain what school to apply to, try the Counselor-O-Matic, which helps you discover schools that are a good fit for you and your goals. Helpful articles provide a variety of information on admissions, testing, and financial aid. While visiting, also work on your test-taking skills with free online practice tests (SAT, ACT, and more) after you register. Or search the scholarship and financial aid database and store your results for future reference.

RWM Vocational School Database

www.rwm.org/rwm

This handy little site provides contact information for private postsecondary vocational schools in all 50 states, including private schools that offer certificate, bachelor's, master's, and doctorate degrees in various academic, business, trade, and technical disciplines. Schools must be state-accredited or licensed. The database is organized by state and then by 22 vocational training fields, ranging from aircraft to welding. It also includes schools that offer online degree and certification programs for students who need to learn from home.

Trade-School.org

www.tradeschool.org

> There are hundreds of trade schools all across the U.S. , each one offering vocational training in a wide variety of specific fields. Trade schools are an attractive option for people who know what they want to be (such as a cosmetologist or an auto mechanic); want the training, skills, and certification required to become what they want to be; but don't want to spend a lot of time and money getting there. Trade-schools.org is a practical, bare-bones site that can help you search for and research schools by state or by popular trade (design schools, culinary schools, business schools, and so on). While there you can read up on the latest trade school news, but that's where the bells and whistles end.

U.S. Universities

www.usuniversities.com

> U.S. Universities allows you to search by state and/or degree program. Each listing contains contact information, a description of the school, and a listing of its programs, as well as a link to e-mail the university for more information. The site also contains a useful section on studying abroad, which you can search by country and/or subject. The site has separate directories for volunteer and teaching opportunities, overseas jobs, high school students interested in foreign programs, and overseas internships.

Web U.S. Higher Education

www.utexas.edu/world/univ

> This directory provides links to U.S. universities and community colleges that are regionally accredited. You can browse the list alphabetically or by state. Updated monthly, What's New shows the latest changes to the list. This site is simple and straightforward.

Apply Online!

Many individual schools let you apply online, but the following sites let you complete common application information and reuse it for multiple applications—saving you time and typing.

CollegeNET

www.collegenet.com/about/index_html

> CollegeNET lets you complete, file, and pay for admissions applications over the Internet for more than 1,500 colleges and universities. It uses a customized Web application that allows common data to travel automatically from form to form, saving you time when filling out forms. To help you figure out where to apply, CollegeNET provides direct access to searches for national two- and four-year schools, vocational/technical and business schools, upper-level undergraduate programs, and nursing programs. Read about tuition, contact information, deadlines, and admission requirements, and then choose your type of application. Financial aid links and a scholarship search help you find funding after you apply. Avoid the home page, however, as it is cluttered and confusing.

Common Application

www.commonapp.org

> Nearly 350 colleges and universities have chosen to standardize the common application, allowing applicants to apply to any of these schools by filling out just one form. Complete the application online or download and print the form in .pdf (Adobe Acrobat—www.adobe.com) format. You can also find brief information on each participating school and a link to its Web site and e-mail address.

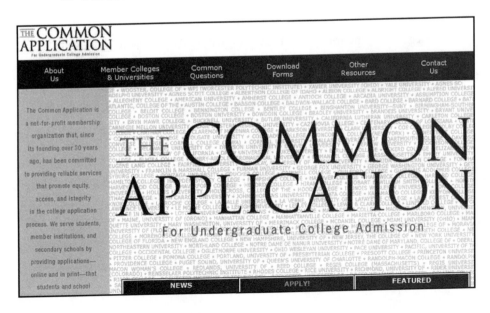

Getting the Scoop on College Entrance Exams

So you've finally narrowed it down to your top few choices—but don't forget that most schools require you to take one or more entrance exams. The following sites help you find out about common tests, register for them, and sign up for test-preparation courses online. Note that some sites mentioned earlier in this chapter, such as Petersons.com and The Princeton Review, are also good sources of testing information and resources.

ACT
www.actstudent.org

Learn what to do before, during, and after taking the ACT, one of the most commonly required examinations for college applicants. You can register online, receive your scores online, learn how scores are reported, register to retake the exam, and have your results sent to additional schools. You can purchase an online test preparation program or book, or take advantage of the free booklets, sample tests, test descriptions, and test tips. Besides test-taking advice, there's information on financial aid, college, and career planning.

College Board
www.collegeboard.com

Register online for the SAT, PSAT/NMSQT, CLEP, and AP exams. Exam descriptions and sample test questions help you prepare for the tests, or you can purchase test-taking software or books. Students with disabilities can find out about requesting accommodations for certain tests. Additional information on this site helps you plan for college, choose a school, and find out about financial aid options. This site also comes in a Spanish-language version. A particularly fun feature is The Official SAT Question of the Day (http://apps.collegeboard.com/qotd/question.do?src=R&questionId=802), which will help you fit in a little practice each day.

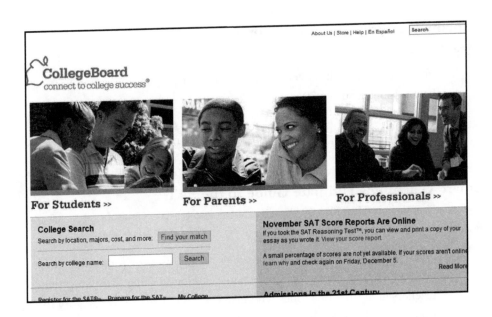

ETS (Educational Testing Service)

www.ets.org

> At ETS, you can quickly link to information on popular tests like the GRE, SAT, and AP exams, or the Teaching of English as a Foreign Language (TOEFL) exam. If testing is in your future, try some sample questions online. Whether you're a student, parent, educator, researcher, or policymaker, ETS has some suggested resources for you.

FairTest: The National Center for Fair and Open Testing

www.fairtest.org/univ/optional.htm

> The secret is out: More than 700 colleges and universities nationwide admit a substantial number of students without regard for their ACT or SAT test score. You can find every one of these schools at this site. The list includes a wide variety of institutions, from small, private liberal arts colleges to large, public university systems. Some of the schools require all applicants to submit test scores whether or not they use the test scores to make admissions decisions. The complete state-by-state list indicates to what extent the schools use the admissions tests, which some studies have shown to be inaccurate predictors of college success.

Kaplan: Test Prep and Admissions

www.kaptest.com

> For years, Kaplan has been known for its test-preparation courses. At kaptest.com, you can sign up to take onsite or online test preparation courses for entrance exams (for a fee), or take advantage of the site's free services. You'll see sample test questions, a variety of e-mail newsletters, and articles on applying to, paying for, and succeeding in college.

Smart Teaching's Ultimate Guide to the SAT

www.smartteaching.org/blog/2008/09/the-ultimate-guide-to-the-sat-100-helpful-sites-and-resources/

> Smart Teaching bills itself as "a leading online resource for current teachers, and aspiring education students and student teachers." But aspiring teachers aren't the only ones who take the SAT. Browse by category to find helpful links on vocabulary building, practice tests, prep books, and general advice on just about everything SAT. The guide is easy to navigate and free to all. As an added bonus, if you are interested in becoming a teacher you can use Smart Teaching's degree finder to research education programs near you.

Your Money's Worth: College Rankings

U.S. News & World Report each year ranks the best colleges and graduate programs in a number of categories. A number of other magazines and Web sites have begun creating their own similar rankings. Although these are always somewhat subjective, rankings are a starting point to help you identify good schools to investigate further.

College Prowler College Rankings

http://collegeprowler.com/colleges/rankings/

> If you want the inside scoop on what a college is really like, there's no better resource than the students themselves. College Prowler is the only guide to colleges written for students, by students. It isn't affiliated with

any particular university, and it provides unique "insider" information that most college guides won't. Its college rankings grade schools on the 20 categories most relevant to college students. Categories range from the traditional—Academics, Athletics, Diversity—to the more social—Nightlife, Local Atmosphere, and Campus Dining. Written by students, some of the information here may be a little more subjective than in other guides, but that also makes it more comprehensive. This site doesn't just tell you whether the school you are interested in has a good reputation or a high graduation rate; it will tell you whether the school is a good fit for you in every aspect of your life. The rankings are free, but you can also buy a subscription to read its college guides, comprehensive descriptions of each college from the students who attend.

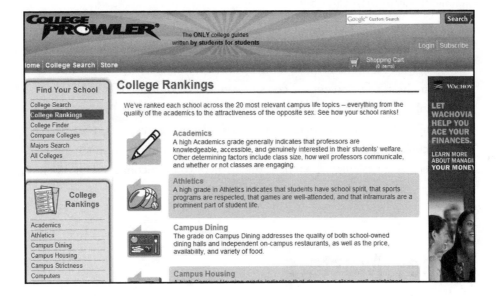

College and University Rankings (UIUC)

www.library.uiuc.edu/edx/rankings.htm

The Education and Social Science Library at the University of Illinois Urbana-Champaign (UIUC) provides a large list of categorized links to college rankings, from undergraduate institutions to law schools. Even better, the site discusses how to understand and interpret the rankings so that you know how much weight to give them. Use this site to locate lists of colleges that are a best value, disability-friendly schools, and more.

Kiplinger's 100 Best Values in Public Colleges

www.kiplinger.com/tools/colleges/

> Going to college is a serious financial investment, one that continues to increase in cost. Leave it to the financial experts at Kiplinger's to help you find a quality college that will fit your pocketbook. You can search its list by overall rank (in-state and out-of-state), enrollment, graduation rate, total cost, percent of cost met by financial aid, even the average debt students at each school graduate with. Although most of the data comes from Peterson's (see earlier entry), Kiplinger's has done the work of finding the best schools for your budget.

USNews.com Education

www.usnews.com/sections/rankings

> Known for its rankings, *U.S. News* presents several of them here: rankings for universities and liberal arts colleges by region; graduate school rankings for several fields, including business, law, medicine, and public affairs; and best-value rankings. Access to some of the information is restricted unless you pay a fee, but there's still plenty of good stuff for free, including a Student Center that offers college planner worksheets, a searchable scholarship database, a personality quiz, a college tuition planner, a loan repayment calculator, online forums where you can connect with others, and more.

Money Matters

Scholarships, loans, and savings plans are all important components of paying for a college education. The following sites help you identify your financial aid options—and, if it's early enough, get started with saving. Many also include additional information on choosing, applying to, and getting through school.

Adventures In Education

http://adventuresineducation.org

> Sponsored by the Texas Guaranteed Student Loan Corporation, Adventures In Education provides information in English and Spanish for prospective college students. Helpful worksheets, Internet links, and clear

instructions help you choose and apply to schools, pay for college, select a career path, find a job after graduation, and manage your money. If you're planning on attending college soon, a handy financial aid calendar keeps you from overlooking important dates in the application process.

America's CareerInfoNet: Scholarship Search

www.acinet.org/acinet/scholarshipsearch/

One of the many tools in America's CareerInfoNet (see chapter 3 for more) is this database of more than 5,000 scholarships, fellowships, loans, and other financial aid opportunities. Start with the Scholarship Search Help for pointers on using the system, which requires no registration or fee.

College Answer

www.collegeanswer.com

Get a head start on preparing for the world of continuing education through this Web site from Sallie Mae. Step-by-step instructions for students (and parents) in English or Spanish walk you through the college selection, application, decision, and financing process. Other helpful tools include an easy-to-use family of calculators for savings, budgeting, and loan repayment, and a school affordability analyzer.

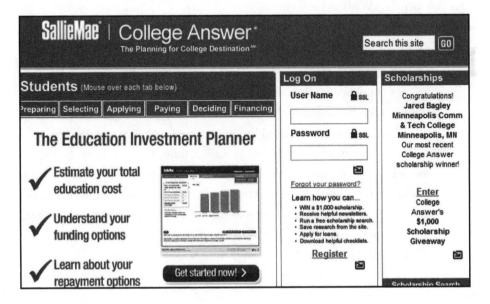

College Is Possible

www.collegeispossible.org

College Is Possible is a national education campaign by the Coalition of America's Colleges and Universities to help address concerns about funding a college education for youth who are underrepresented in post-secondary education. Find out what educational institutions in your state participate in the program. Information here includes how to prepare for, choose, and pay for college, with a special section geared toward adult students.

College Savings Plans Network

www.collegesavings.org

All 50 states offer the 529 college savings plan (named after the part of the IRS code that authorizes them), and this site links to information on each state's unique programs. You'll find out about the 529 savings program, which allows families to put aside federal tax-exempt savings for college or purchase prepaid, locked-in tuition to state schools. The College Savings Plans Network was formed in 1991 as an affiliate to the National Association of State Treasurers to make higher education more attainable.

FAFSA on the Web

www.fafsa.ed.gov

The Free Application for Federal Student Aid, fondly known as the FAFSA, is required for any student who wants federal assistance. The process is not speedy, but the site does an excellent job of laying out the steps to take, in English or Spanish. The hardest part may be gathering the financial information you need before you begin, like income tax return and bank statements, but the site lists all of those for you. Even better, the online application process lets you store your partially completed form so that you can finish it later if you're missing some required information. You can get your application processed the fastest by submitting it online, which requires obtaining an electronic personal identification number (PIN). Again, instructions here tell you how.

FastWeb

www.fastweb.com

> FastWeb is one of the most reputable Internet scholarship search services. However, you must enter extensive information about yourself if you want to use it, including your age, mailing address, ethnicity, career objectives, academic background, student activities, and your parents' activities. The site uses this data to generate a personalized suite of information on colleges, internships, jobs, and scholarships, which number over 1.3 million and are worth more than $3 billion. FastWeb is a Monster company.

Federal Student Aid

www.studentaid.ed.gov

> For the official word on student financial assistance, turn to this site from the U.S. Department of Education. Organized in a very user-friendly manner to help you find the information you need, the site walks you through the financial steps of preparing, choosing, applying, funding, attending, and repaying. Learn where to begin whether you are in elementary school, junior high, high school, college, or graduate school, or if you are a returning student, international student, parent, or counselor. Information here includes descriptions of the different federal student aid programs and eligibility requirements, help in choosing your ideal college, a financial aid wizard to help calculate your college costs, and much more. Learn about the process for applying online for financial aid, and then go do it at FAFSA on the Web (described a couple of paragraphs ago). Last but not least, the information here on repaying, consolidating, or finding forgiveness programs for existing loans is useful for graduates.

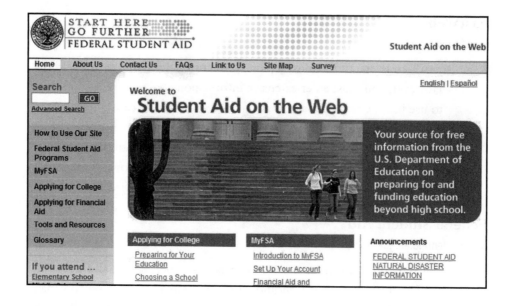

FinAid!

www.finaid.org

Established in 1994, this award-winning site remains the most comprehensive online clearinghouse on funding a college education. Choose from loans, scholarships, military aid, and other types of aid to learn about all your options, and then check out extra tools such as links to financial aid applications, calculators, and personalized advice. FinAid! is also a part of Monster.

Hispanic Scholarship Fund (HSF)

www.hsf.net

HSF is the nation's leading organization supporting Hispanic higher education. HSF was founded in 1975 with a vision to strengthen the country by advancing college education among Hispanic Americans—the largest minority segment of the U.S. population. Since then, HSF has awarded more than 86,000 scholarships totaling nearly $247 million to Latinos from all 50 states who have attended 2,000 colleges and universities. The site provides information on scholarship eligibility, application, and selection.

Mapping Your Future

www.mappingyourfuture.biz/

Although Mapping Your Future provides information on the career-planning process, the main focus of this site is selecting and paying for college. Get started by taking a guided tour based on your category—middle or high school student, undergraduate, adult student, parent, counselor, and so on. Special features include online loan counseling interviews, financial fitness guides and calculators, scheduled interactive chat sessions on financial aid topics, and information on selecting and working toward a career.

MyRichUncle

https://www.myrichuncle.com

If you can't cover the cost of your education through financial aid or parental aid, learn about private lending from MyRichUncle. Get informed about things like APR, origination fees, and capitalization, and then decide if a private loan should be part of your school finance plan. If you like what you see, you can apply online for private, internship, or study-abroad loans.

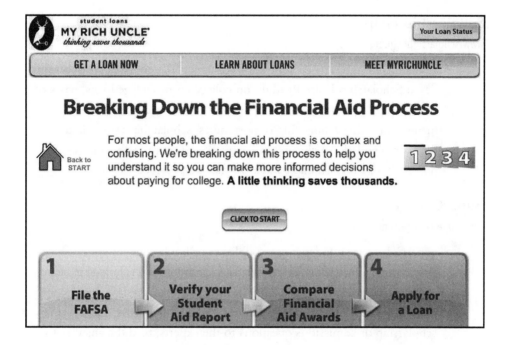

Nellie Mae

www.nelliemae.com

> Nellie Mae, a wholly owned subsidiary of SLM Corporation (Sallie Mae, described next), allows you to apply or prequalify online for student loans. In many cases it provides an instantaneous response. You'll learn about the different types of loans that are offered, including requirements, fees, interest rates, and repayment options. Calculators help you compare award letters, set up a budget, calculate accrued interest on unsubsidized loans, compute prepayment savings, and more. The Educational Investment Planner can help you estimate your costs, understand your options, and choose the one that is best for you.

Sallie Mae

www.salliemae.com

> Sallie Mae, the leading provider of education loans, primarily funds federally guaranteed student loans. Here you can find information to help you prepare for, select, apply to, and finance college. This Web site also includes information for students on how to manage their loans once they graduate.

Scholarship Help

www.scholarshiphelp.org

> Learn the ins and outs of applying for a variety of scholarship opportunities at Scholarship Help. Read up on college costs, college loans, types of scholarships, how scholarship applications are judged, personal assessments, evaluating scholarship opportunities, scholarship essays, letters of recommendation, scholarship renewals, and more. Although this site doesn't have a scholarship database, links are provided to several.

SuperCollege

www.supercollege.com

> SuperCollege is an independent publisher of books and resources on college planning, including this Web site. In addition to a scholarship search (after you register for free), you'll find features organized for high school, college, and graduate students, parents, and adult students. Submit your scholarship or admissions questions to the experts, read the answers to

questions submitted by others, or subscribe to the free scholarship and admissions newsletters.

United Negro College Fund (UNCF)
www.uncf.org

UNCF is the nation's largest, oldest, most successful, and most comprehensive minority higher education assistance organization. UNCF provides operating funds and technology enhancement services for 39 historically black colleges and universities, scholarships and internships for students at about 900 institutions, and faculty and administrative professional training. The searchable database includes scholarships from UNCF and other organizations. If you're a student at a UNCF member college, filling out a profile is optional but highly recommended.

Interstate Student Exchange Programs

The following boards and commission sponsor programs that allow students to pursue degrees (in specified majors) at out-of-state institutions at less than the normal out-of-state tuition. This can result in significant savings if you want to attend school in another state. If you just want to study elsewhere in the U.S. or Canada for a year, there's a site for that too.

Midwestern Higher Education Compact (MHEC) Midwest Student Exchange Program
http://msep.mhec.org

The Midwest Student Exchange Program of the Midwestern Higher Education Compact (MHEC) serves students from Kansas, Michigan, Minnesota, Missouri, Nebraska, North Dakota, and Wisconsin. Through the program, public institutions agree to charge students no more than 150 percent of the in-state resident tuition rate for specific programs; private institutions offer a 10 percent reduction on their tuition rates. The site lists more than 125 participating colleges and universities, plus you can search by type of degree and school. Locate contacts for the participating states, or download a PDF brochure with all the information.

National Student Exchange

www.nse.org

> If you long to expand your horizons but studying abroad is beyond your
> reach, check out the National Student Exchange. The program helps stu-
> dents study in other parts of the U.S. and Canada for up to one academic
> year. Students pay either their normal tuition and fees at the home campus
> or the in-state tuition and fees at their host campus. Since the program
> began 40 years ago, more than 90,000 students have used the program to
> broaden their academic careers.

NSE provides students with affordable and practical opportunities

New England Board of Higher Education (NEBHE) Tuition Assistance

www.nebhe.org

> If you're a resident of Connecticut, Maine, Massachusetts, New Hampshire,
> Rhode Island, or Vermont, the New England Regional Student Program
> (RSP) might save you money. Sponsored by the New England Board of
> Higher Education (NEBHE), the RSP provides a tuition break for stu-
> dents to study certain majors (that are not available at public colleges in
> their own states) at public colleges and universities in other New England
> states. Majors at all levels of study and participating institutions are listed in

each year's RSP catalog, which you can download. You can also search the online database of programs and participating institutions.

Southern Regional Education Board (SREB) Academic Common Market

www.sreb.org/programs/acm/acmindex.asp

> Through the Southern Regional Education Board (SREB) Academic Common Market program, residents can pursue unique majors at regional public institutions outside their home states while paying in-state tuition. You can even take distance courses through the SREB's Electronic Campus (described in chapter 2) under certain conditions, explained here. You also find out about the SREB Regional Contract Program, which gives out-of-state tuition breaks to students pursuing professional health degrees in fields such as dentistry and optometry. SREB's 16 member states are Alabama, Arkansas, Delaware, Florida, Georgia, Kentucky, Louisiana, Maryland, Mississippi, North Carolina, Oklahoma, South Carolina, Tennessee, Texas, Virginia, and West Virginia. Check the SREB Web site for more information, including contacts for specific programs in each state.

Western Interstate Commission for Higher Education (WICHE) Student Exchange Programs

www.wiche.edu/SEP

> Students in Alaska, Arizona, California, Colorado, Hawaii, Idaho, Montana, Nevada, New Mexico, North Dakota, Oregon, South Dakota, Utah, Washington, and Wyoming can participate in this exchange program, which offers significant savings on out-of-state tuition among these Western states. Undergraduates, graduate students, and professional students can find out if their field of study is supported, find a list of schools, and learn how to apply.

Choosing a College Major

It might not be a decision you are ready for, or it might be one that you made when you were only eight years old. Still, the choice of college major is also, quite often, the choice of career. What we want to be will have a direct impact on what we will need to study. That means you should spend as much time choosing and researching your major or program of study as you would your choice of career. Not to mention that making an informed decision about a major from the get-go can save you a lot of time and money. The following sites can help.

Majors and Careers Central: CollegeBoard

www.collegeboard.com/student/csearch/majors_careers/index.html

There are many reasons to get a college degree, but most people do it with the hopes of advancing or expanding their careers. Since a choice of college major often dictates the kinds of career opportunities that become available after graduation, it's a good idea to research majors that you are interested in and see how, exactly, they connect to careers. This database run by the CollegeBoard provides overviews of more than 600 majors. You can search by major category or by career category. All majors include a basic description of the major and links to related majors and careers, and many also offer college checklists, course spotlights, and other tips that will help you decide whether the major is right for you. From there you can link to a wide variety of occupational information resources to see what prospects that major will open up. An overall useful site for making the connection between college and career.

MyMajors.com

www.mymajors.com

For most students, the choice of major plays a significant role in the choice of school. But many incoming students don't know what they want to major in. MyMajors.com can help. Start by taking the survey to match your interests and achievements to your top five majors. If you already know what program you are interested in, go to the Major Information Pages where majors are listed within their academic disciplines. Clicking on each major takes you to an in-depth description of that major along with links to universities to consider. Taking the MyMajors quiz is free, but it will require you to register. Be sure to read the Terms and Conditions before you get started.

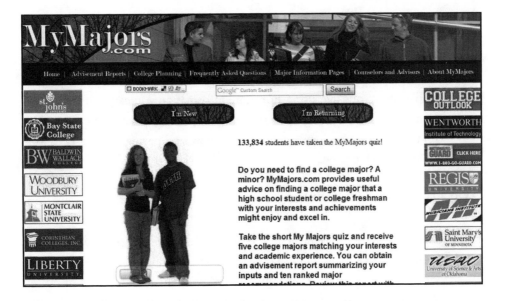

General Information on Postsecondary Education

You'll find even more information on all aspects of postsecondary education at the next few sites.

Back to College

www.back2college.com

> If you're an adult entering college for the first time or you want to finish that degree you started years ago, this site is for you. Back to College contains information and links to topics from admissions to financial aid to finding a program. "Ask the Experts" your questions about going back to college, or talk with other returnees in the online forums. You can also sign up for a free monthly e-mail newsletter.

College Confidential

http://talk.collegeconfidential.com/

> Need someone to talk to about the college admissions process? College Confidential is the Web's leading discussion forum for college admissions, including information on financial aid, SAT preparation, and much more.

Joining the free community will let you post topics and message with other members, although you can still read the discussion boards without registering. As with all discussion forums, there is a lot to sift through, but topics are well organized and most members are more than happy to help answer your questions. For more information you can visit College Confidential's home page at www.collegeconfidential.com. Here you can find articles on choosing a college, getting in, and paying for it, as well as a college search engine.

HEATH Resource Center

www.heath.gwu.edu

George Washington University's HEATH Resource Center serves as a comprehensive clearinghouse on postsecondary education for students with disabilities. Browse the extensive links for annotated listings of related Web sites and organizations by topic areas, or read the quarterly newsletter and other free publications.

Students.gov

www.students.gov

Students.gov is a comprehensive information portal from the U.S. government on topics of interest to students. These include education, career development, military service, community service, and travel. The education sections provide links to choosing a college, testing, scholarships and grants, loan repayment, state financial aid, and more. Everything is searchable in case you're looking for something specific. Just use the "I want to…" drop-down box to find what you need.

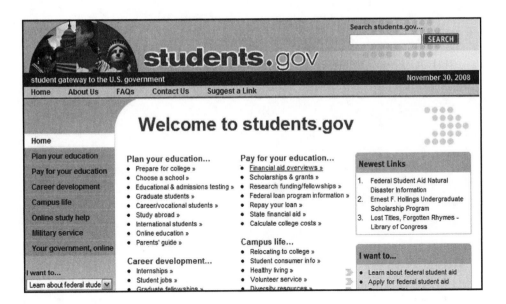

U.S. Department of Education

www.ed.gov

> Links on the main page of the U.S. Department of Education's Web site help you quickly locate information of interest to you, whether you are a student, parent, teacher, or administrator. You can get an overview of federal student aid, find links for planning for college or technical training, identify graduate student resources, locate information on studying abroad, and much more. You can also download popular publications such as the yearly Student Guide to Financial Aid. The site also offers education resources for Spanish speakers.

Zinch

www.zinch.com

> Most college recruiting is done by test score. A high score on the SAT may lead to an application to Harvard appearing in your mailbox. Zinch tries to improve upon this overly simplistic process by letting high school students create a profile—a kind of student portfolio—that colleges can then use to make more effective and informed recruiting and admission decisions. The process is straightforward: students create an online portfolio using Zinch's easy profile creator. You can upload examples of your writing, art, music, school projects, you name it. Colleges and universities

then search through the database to find students that match their mission and standards. With more than 611 colleges currently recruiting 400,000 high school students with profiles already, it can't hurt to take a look and create a portfolio of your own.

Distance Learning and Lifelong Learning

Whether you want to complete a college degree or take a personal enrichment course, opportunities for learning without leaving your home continue to increase every year. *Distance learning* has become less novel and more mainstream for several reasons. Computers have gotten faster and less expensive, plus high-speed Internet access is now widely available and affordable. More schools and institutions of higher learning are offering more courses, and they're getting better at it. In fact, the Distance Education Clearinghouse (described in this chapter) lists training programs for distance educators.

Ongoing learning is critical in the workplace, where employers face the need to maintain a well-trained staff and employees need to sharpen their skills to stay current or get ahead in their fields. For many, the availability and convenience of distance learning is hard to beat.

However, distance education carries a price tag. Like any educational program, distance learning is an investment of your time and money. The Web sites in this chapter have been reviewed and selected to help you become a wise investor in distance learning.

Here are a few suggestions: Take the SORT assessment (described at the end of the next section) to help determine if distance learning is right for you. Search several sites to find the programs you're most interested in. No one directory lists all available programs. Do a little research on the employment outlook for the career you're exploring (see chapter 3) to be sure your investment can pay off. In my research, I spotted an online training course for TV/VCR repair—no doubt a declining occupation. Finally, be sure you know the total cost of your program of study. Some sites list costs by semester, and others by credit hour. Do the math yourself. Take advantage of any distance education advising a school or consortium offers prospective students to get the answers you need.

Learning About Distance Learning

Before you take the plunge, find out more about what you may be getting into. A little time spent investigating these sites can pay off in the long run.

About Distance Learning

http://distancelearn.about.com

> About.com's distance learning section has a nice selection of general distance learning articles and resources—if you don't mind reading around ads that take up screen space. Articles on choosing a distance learning school, paying for school, and more are loaded with plenty of links for further research.

DegreeInfo.com

www.degreeinfo.com

> DegreeInfo.com began as "a place where people genuinely interested in quality distance learning programs can come to discuss, learn, share, and help one another." The site started out as an active discussion board on distance learning, and that remains its outstanding feature. Read what others have to say about distance learning, or post a question yourself.

Distance Education Clearinghouse

www.uwex.edu/disted/index.cfm

> The University of Wisconsin–Extension provides the Distance Education Clearinghouse, a comprehensive, up-to-date directory of online resources on distance learning. Geared toward teachers, institutions, and students alike, its clearly annotated links (found on the right side of the screen) are broken into a number of useful categories, including programs and courses,

technology, teaching and learning, research and statistics, distance education community, and more. If you discover you really enjoy distance learning, there's a listing of certificate programs so that you can train to become an instructor yourself.

geteducated.com

www.geteducated.com/index.asp

Get educated about online education here. GetEducated.com's mission is to operate the only clearinghouse in the U.S. dedicated to showcasing accredited online degrees. Accreditation is important if you want a public record of your learning that will be widely accepted by employers, professional associations, and other colleges and universities. This site has surveys of top business and computer majors, "best buy" rankings for selected online programs, and free downloadable e-books listing accredited schools offering graduate and undergraduate degrees in specific areas.

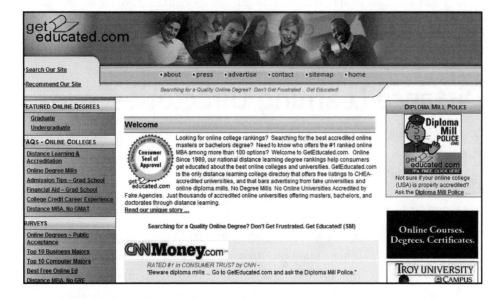

Online Education Blog

www.onlineedublog.com/

OnlineEduBlog is primarily a database of online colleges that you can search by subject or degree, on-campus, off-campus, or both. It offers comprehensive reviews of the colleges it lists and includes only accredited institutions. Search for colleges that interest you, read the brief descriptions, and check out the list of programs; then follow a link to the college itself. When you've finished your search, you can join the community to share information and experiences with other distance-learning students. Check out the News and Reviews tab for the latest information about online education or take a quiz to see whether distance learning is right for you or whether you are on the right career path.

University System of Georgia's Student Online Readiness Tool (SORT)

www.alt.usg.edu/sort/html/sortlau1.html

According to research, six main topics are closely related to a student's success in the online learning environment. SORT helps you rate yourself in each of these areas. Based on your responses to questions, you receive feedback on your personal readiness profile, along with suggested strategies for success and links to more information. Make this site a prerequisite before you sign up for any distance learning training.

Distance Learning Directories

Distance learning directories gather and organize distance learning offerings to make it easier for you to find what interests you.

Degree.net

www.degree.net

This companion Web site to Bears' Guide to Earning Degrees by Distance Learning and other distance learning guides includes columns, news stories, links to other distance education sites, and much more. Be sure to investigate the extensive accreditation information to get the background you need to evaluate distance learning schools and courses.

GradSchools.com

www.gradschools.com/online-programs.html

As you might guess from the name, this site specializes in graduate school information, and the link provided above takes you directly to their data on distance learning programs. Distance graduate programs make it easier for adults with work and/or family responsibilities to earn graduate degrees from home, or by spending limited time on campus. GradSchools. com let's you search a comprehensive list of programs of study and academic areas. Each school listing contains contact information as well as several links to the school's Web site for further information on the program.

EarnMyDegree

www.earnmydegree.com/

EarnMyDegree.com has connected more than 3 million students to adult online education programs. It does so with an easy-to-use, multifaceted search engine that allows you to research colleges by subject, degree level, or location. Your search will bring up information about the programs available and the schools that offer them, along with links to request even more information. You can also search for online courses—if you wanted to learn more about catering or real estate, for example. EarnMyDegree also offers an online learning center, which includes its online education guide, as well as other articles on education and career topics. A very useful site for students who are unsure whether online learning is right for them and want to know just what they are getting into.

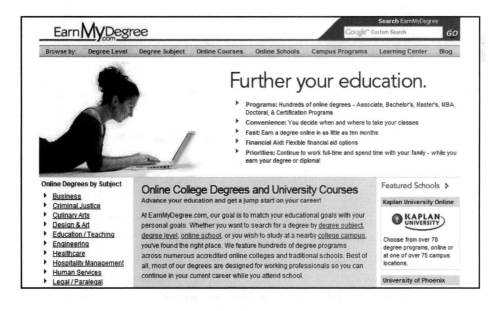

GuideToOnlineSchools.com

www.guidetoonlineschools.com

> The name speaks for itself in this easy-to-search directory of more than 2,500 online degree programs. In addition to its searchable database, it offers an extensive Educational Resources section with accreditation and financial aid information. The site also includes reviews written by actual students who have attended the universities listed on the site.

Petersons.com: Online Learning

www.petersons.com/distancelearning/

> This page from Petersons.com provides an online search for hundreds of distance learning programs. You can search institutions by name, by degree programs, by degree programs without on-campus requirements, or by courses. You'll find detailed descriptions of most of the colleges, as well as contact information and links to their Web sites. See chapter 1 for more on Petersons.com.

USNews.com: Education: E-Learning

www.usnews.com/sections/education/e-learning/index.html

> USNews.com's searchable e-learning directory includes more than 2,800 regionally accredited institutions offering distance course work for credit. Unlike most other directories, which require you to contact the school for financial information, USNews.com lists per-credit costs and the availability of financial aid for distance learning.

WorldWideLearn

www.worldwidelearn.com

> World Wide Learn has both online and on-campus directories, but since we're talking about distance learning, here's the scoop: World Wide Learn features both online degree programs and online nondegree courses. The degree programs are organized by type of degree, from high school through doctorate. Nondegree courses range from business skills and vocational training to foreign languages. So whether you're committed to a program or you just want to get your toes wet, this site is a good place to explore. You can also subscribe to the WorldWideBlog at www.worldwidelearn.com/worldwideblog/ for more frequent updates and entertaining issues regarding distance education.

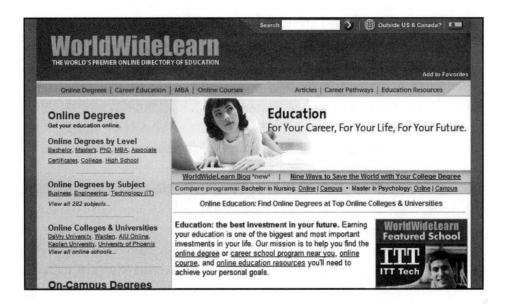

Distance Learning Career and Degree Institutions

This section offers a closer look at some institutions that offer distance learning programs. These examples show a nice range of possibilities, from high school diploma programs to vocational training to graduate degrees.

Capella University

www.capella.edu

> With nearly 24,000 students earning their degrees online, 1,000 courses, and 22 degree programs to choose from, Capella is one of the leaders in delivering online education. Visit the Cost and Financing page to get an estimate of what a degree might cost, browse the video testimonials of students at the university, or request a university guide by e-mail. For an even more in-depth tour, follow the Online Learning link for access inside Capella's virtual classrooms. View a short course demo or sign up for a free one-week online seminar. This is a great way to see whether distance learning in general, and Capella University specifically, is right for you. With programs from the certificate level all the way up to Ph.D., most adult learners can find a way to advance their educations here.

Center for Distance and Independent Study: University of Missouri–Columbia (CDIS)

http://cdis.missouri.edu/

Want an accredited four-year diploma—your high school diploma, that is? The Center for Distance and Independent Study of the University of Missouri–Columbia offers accredited high school courses for independent learners. Take courses online and apply the credit at your own high school, investigate classes not available in your area, catch up on courses, find courses for gifted students, supplement a home-schooling curriculum, or earn your diploma entirely online. If you qualify academically, you may even enroll in university-level courses offered through CDIS while paying only 50 percent of the normal University of Missouri educational fees. CDIS also offers middle-school courses and a bachelor of general studies degree program.

Jones International University (JIU)

www.jonesinternational.edu

Jones International, the first accredited fully online university, offers undergraduate, graduate, and certificate programs with focuses on business and education. Its programs are developed and supported by content experts who are some of the most highly respected authorities in their fields. Each new student receives an online orientation to JIU, including instruction on using class Web pages and discussion forums, and peer and academic advisors are available via e-mail. JIU makes a strong effort to make education affordable, with several financial assistance programs and tuition payment options. It also offers credit for prior learning. This site is also available in Spanish.

Kaplan University

www.kaplan.edu

Kaplan does more than prep high school students for the SATs. As part of Kaplan Higher Education—with more than 70 campuses across 20 states—Kaplan University is one of the largest online colleges in the world. The university offers degree programs in 11 areas of study, many of them leading directly to in-demand careers. Its online degree programs include interactive seminars with other students, online quizzes, discussion boards, interactive (online) field trips, and one-on-one teacher/student feedback. To learn more, download the catalog or engage in a live chat with one of Kaplan's admissions counselors.

National University

www.nu.edu

Operated out of California and accredited by the Western Association of Schools and Colleges, National University has a wide variety of undergraduate and graduate programs available online. Programs include Business and Management, Education, Engineering and Technology, Health and Human Services, Media and Communication, and the College of Letters and Sciences. National's courses are taught in a unique one-course-per-month format, so you stay focused on one class at a time and move through them quickly to earn your degree faster. With more than 1,200 courses available online, it's worth checking to see what programs they have available.

Penn Foster Career School

www.pennfoster.edu

Penn Foster specializes in distance career programs for adult learners and offers a wide range of options, from child day care management to court reporter to motorcycle repair technician. Penn Foster also offers a high school degree program as well as associate's degrees in selected areas. Choose an area of interest to receive a free information packet by mail, and then enroll in a program to receive self-study materials at home. Proceed through modules and take exams online, by mail, or by phone at your own pace.

University of Phoenix

www.phoenix.edu

If you spend enough time online, you are bound to see an advertisement for this school. The nation's largest private university with more than 300,000 students, the University of Phoenix gears its accredited graduate and undergraduate degree programs toward working adults. You can learn entirely online; take in-person courses near you at one of their nearly 200 campuses across the U.S., Canada, Puerto Rico, and Mexico; or use a combination of both to complete your degree. Browse the site to find out about degrees offered, tuition costs, and financial aid.

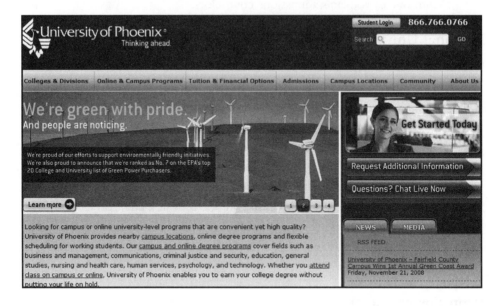

University of Texas (UT)

www.telecampus.utsystem.edu

UT offers undergraduate degrees, master's degrees, and certificate programs, all online. You'll also find a searchable database of classes offered by any UT campus through any distance education method. Online professional development courses are available here as well.

Walden University

www.waldenu.edu

Walden University offers programs in eight academic areas: education, management, psychology, nursing, health sciences, counseling and social service, public policy and administration, and engineering and applied science. In addition, Walden's dual degree options allow you to expand the breadth of your learning and earn two degrees in less time than if you pursued each separately.

Western Governors University

www.wgu.edu/index.asp

> Founded by the governors of several western states, Western Governors'
> program uses a unique competency-based (rather than credit-based) sys-
> tem. The programs are not based upon required courses. Instead, you earn
> your degree by demonstrating your competence through a series of care-
> fully designed assessments—an approach that allows for extensive person-
> alization. Program offerings include education, business, and information
> technology.

Distance Learning Consortia

State or regional distance learning consortia harness the power of multiple institutions to provide a broad array of classes and options to potential students, generally allowing students enrolled in one of the schools to take distance education
courses at any other member institution. Again, these are just examples of the
variety of consortia available. Find out whether your own state or regional board
sponsors its own version.

Canadian Virtual University (CVU)

www.cvu-uvc.ca

> The 12 universities in this consortium offer 300 complete degrees, diplo-
> mas, and certificates. More than 2,500 individual courses are available
> completely online or through distance education. Most, but not all, of the
> courses are open to international (non-Canadian) students. Search here for
> degree programs or for individual courses in your area of interest. Degrees
> are provided through your accredited "home university" rather than
> through CVU itself. This site is available in both English and French.

The College Network (TCN)

www.college-net.com/

> If you're an adult with work and life experience, take a look at the pro-
> grams offered through the College Network. TCN works with its fully
> accredited partner institutions to help students earn up to 82 credits by

testing out of prerequisites and general-education courses. Earn your associate's, bachelor's, or master's degree or professional certificate in less time than you anticipated. Programs of study include business, criminal justice, engineering, health care, human resources, nursing, and more.

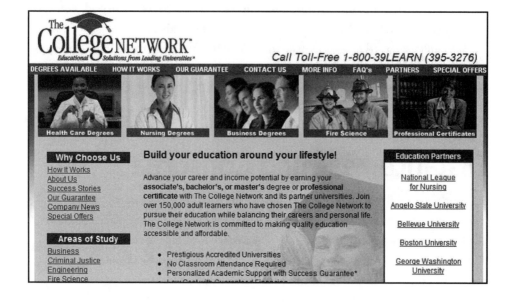

Electronic Campus (Southern Regional Education Board)

www.electroniccampus.org/AdultLearner/

The Electronic Campus of the Southern Regional Education Board lists information on thousands of distance learning courses and programs for the 16 SREB states. (For more on SREB, see chapter 1.) Fortunately, the site also has powerful search tools to help you easily zoom in on your needs and interests. A number of courses are available at an "electronic tuition rate," which offers significant savings over out-of-state tuition.

National Universities Degree Consortium (NUDC)

www.nudc.org

The National Universities Degree Consortium (NUDC) is a nationwide collaborative of higher-education institutions, offering fully accredited courses and degree programs through eight different universities. Courses are delivered in flexible formats (including the Internet, audio and video, printed self-study materials, CD-ROM, and teleconferences). You can browse by school or degree program, or conduct a keyword search through all the course offerings.

SUNY Learning Network

http://sln.suny.edu/index.html

The State University of New York Learning Network of online programs lists more than 100 degrees and certificate programs with more than 4,300 individual courses. Unlike many other distance learning programs, courses listed here have specific start and end dates, which may be useful if you need help staying on track. Students enroll directly in the institution offering the course or degree they're interested in. Tuition costs vary depending on campus, course level, and residency status.

Continuing Education, at a Distance

No degrees are available from the sites listed here, but if you want to try out a class or two for your own personal development, you're in the right place. Also, keep in mind that many other distance learning institutions allow students to take individual courses without enrolling in a degree program.

MIT OpenCourseWare (OCW)

http://ocw.mit.edu/OcwWeb/

Ever wanted to attend the Massachusetts Institute of Technology, but couldn't afford the tuition? As it turns out, MIT offers noncredit courses free of charge to the public. Courses consist of lecture notes, exams, videos, and other media created by MIT professors. No registration is required. You simply search for the course you want, download the required materials, follow the syllabus, and teach yourself. If MIT isn't your school of choice, try Yale, with courses ranging from Modern Poetry to Frontiers of Biomedical Engineering, all found at http://oyc.yale.edu/.

OnlineLearning.net

www.OnlineLearning.net

> Busy teachers looking to meet professional development continuing-education requirements or lifelong learning objectives should investigate this specialized site's online options. Undergraduate and graduate degrees are not offered here, but you can earn transferable college credit for some of the online courses. You can also sign up with this site to create a personal start page and receive information on new courses and upcoming events.

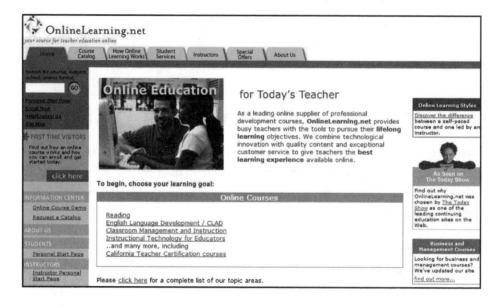

Seminar Information Service

www.seminarinformation.com

> If distance learning isn't your thing, the Seminar Information Service provides an easy way to search for more than 360,000 live, in-person seminars, classes, workshops, conferences, and corporate training events annually. Conduct a quick search by keyword, location, or date, or browse featured events each month. Most seminars provide the option to enroll online.

Teleclass.com

www.teleclass.com

> For a unique experience in distance learning, try Teleclass.com. You register online but classes occur by telephone, allowing you to interact with an

instructor and other students. Classes usually meet once a week for one or two months. However, some are single-session classes, and the best news is that they're often free. Topics generally focus on human development and self-improvement, and range from coaching and consulting to communicating with your teenager to writing a top-notch book proposal.

Military-Sponsored Educational Opportunities

The U.S. military recognizes the importance of education for all service members and sponsors both degree and continuing-education opportunities. A number of these are available online or through other distance learning methods so that active personnel can learn while serving their country, wherever they may be stationed. For information on joining or working for the military, see chapter 6.

Air University

www.au.af.mil/au/

> For a comprehensive look at educational opportunities in the Air Force, visit Air University. Headquartered at Maxwell Air Force Base in Montgomery, Alabama, Air University is the Air Force's center for professional military education. It covers the full spectrum of education, from precommissioning to degree-granting and professional continuing education for officers, enlisted personnel, and civilians throughout their careers.

Community College of the Air Force

www.au.af.mil/au/ccaf/

> The Community College of the Air Force is the only degree-granting institution of higher learning in the world dedicated to enlisted people. CCAF offers unique opportunities for active-duty Air National Guard, Air Force Reserve, and noncommissioned officers to earn a job-related, two-year undergraduate associate's degree in applied science. Thousands have done so. Since issuing its first degree in 1977, the college has awarded more than 275,000 associate degrees in applied science. The site explains how to find out more about distance learning options through affiliated schools.

Credentialing Opportunities On-Line (COOL)

https://www.cool.army.mil/

> Start your planning here for a civilian career. COOL explains how Army soldiers can meet civilian certification and license requirements related to their Military Occupational Specialties (MOSs). Identify civilian licensed occupations similar to your current military work, and learn how to fill the gaps between Army training and experience and civilian job credentials. Go to the COOL Overview for an easy-to-follow first-time visitors' guide to the site.

DANTES Distance Learning Programs

www.dantes.doded.mil

> Through agreements with a number of schools with existing distance learning programs, DANTES provides distance learning opportunities to active service members in all branches of service who are in the process of earning their degrees, wherever they are stationed. Nondegree courses are also available for military personnel looking to improve their technical or other skills. Up to 75% of tuition costs can be reimbursed by DANTES or the appropriate service branch upon successful completion of each course. For some distance learning inspiration, check out the success stories in the monthly DANTES newsletter posted online.

eArmyU.com

www.earmyu.com

eArmyU offers soldiers learning anytime, anywhere, in nearly 150 online degree programs through partnerships with more than 28 U.S. universities. First read over the Tuition Assistance Policies to see whether you qualify for the program. Then browse through the certificates and degrees that are offered, or search the catalog for specific courses in your area of interest. Subjects are broken into several "program communities." Mentors are available to advise students in their areas of study. Army personnel can earn credits, certificates, and degrees at a low cost or no cost while remaining on active duty. Each program enrollee receives a technology package for use in his or her studies, including a laptop preloaded with the appropriate software.

GI Bill

www.gibill.va.gov

Get the official word about the educational benefits offered by the GI Bill at this site. Important announcements are posted right on the front page of the site. Use the FAQ to find quick answers to the most frequently asked questions about the bill, and ask your own question via an online form if it is not answered there. You can also print copies of applications and other useful forms and find current news on rate changes and other program changes.

MarineNet

www.marinenet.usmc.mil

MarineNet is the gateway for online training for members of the Marine Corps. This site offers plenty of information to get you started, such as eligibility, computer requirements, and course descriptions, as well as self-education bonus promotion points and reserve retirement credits. Some courses offer college credit.

Navy College Program

www.navycollege.navy.mil

> The mission of the Navy College Program is to help sailors earn college degrees by providing academic credit for Navy training, work experience, and off-duty education. Find out here about the Navy College Program for Afloat College Education, which offers undergraduate and graduate courses to sailors on sea duty assignments. The NCP Distance Learning Partnership Schools Program, also described here, helps sailors anywhere make maximum use of military professional training and experience to fulfill degree requirements and meet their educational goals.

Servicemembers Opportunity Colleges (SOC)

www.soc.aascu.org

> This consortium of more than 1,800 colleges and universities allows U.S. military service members and their families to complete associate's and bachelor's degrees, no matter where they are stationed or how often they move. Courses are offered at Army, Navy, Marine Corps, and Coast Guard installations or via distance learning. Member colleges have agreed to accept each other's transfer credits. Start by reading "Why Participate in a SOC Program?" (under "For Students") for basic information on SOC advantages and requirements. Then check out the links for each service branch for descriptions of specific programs, or download the current SOC Guide (in Adobe Acrobat format) for information on each participating institution and applicable policies.

U.S. Marine Corps College of Continuing Education

www.tecom.usmc.mil/cce/

> If you're a Marine, learn about the many continuing-education opportunities open to you. In addition to the online learning network, MarineNet (described earlier), the College of Continuing Education offers training through learning resource centers and a video teletraining network. Also find out about the Command and Staff College and Expeditionary Warfare School Distance Education Seminar programs on officer professional military education. Experienced and diverse faculty members include active-duty and reserve Marines, government civilian employees, and contracted adjunct faculty.

CHAPTER 3

Career Exploration Information

With all the career choices available to you, how do you choose? The Web sites in this chapter can help. We've organized them into categories to help you more easily find what you need. If you're just starting to think about a career, begin with the Web sites in the "Career Planning" section to get organized. The "Self-Assessment" sites provide a variety of tools for you to learn more about yourself and why some jobs may appeal to you more than others. The U.S. Department of Labor is an excellent source of a range of helpful information. We'll give you ideas of where to look. The section "State-Based Career Information" tells you how to find such an information system in your state.

And that's just for starters. The "Career Information Potpourri" section is a sampling of Web sites that provide a variety of career information aimed at a range of audiences, from high school students to older workers. We've included online resources for apprenticeship, job training, and salary information. We'll look at job benefits and tell you why being prepared for job loss is a sound career strategy.

Many job and resume banks, such as CareerBuilder and Monster, also feature articles and helpful information on career selection and exploration. Clearinghouses of career-related links are another great resource for identifying general and specific career information on the Web. These sites are grouped in chapter 4.

Career Planning

Career planning is simply a strategy to help you organize your career-selection efforts. There is no right or wrong way to decide which career to pursue. The problem is that so many people just don't know where to start. Here are some ideas.

Career Planning Steps

Every journey begins with a single step. These sites will get you going with practical suggestions and plenty of resources.

Career Development eManual

www.cdm.uwaterloo.ca/index2.asp

> This site is a gem and an excellent place to begin your personal career development process. The Career Development eManual from the staff at the University of Waterloo (Canada) Career Services Office walks you step-by-step through a time-tested planning process, complete with exercises, video interviews, and additional resources. The six steps are Self-Assessment, Research, Decision-Making (including Education), Networks & Contacts, Work, and Life/Work Planning. Packed with information without any distracting ads, this award-winning site provides a real public service.

Career Planning Process

www.bgsu.edu/offices/sa/career/students/page17957.html

> The Career Planning Process from Bowling Green State University in
> Bowling Green, Ohio, outlines a career exploration model to help you
> gain competencies, make decisions, set goals, and take action. The steps
> are Self-Assessment, Academic/Career Options, Relevant/Practical
> Experience, Job Search/Graduate School Preparation, and Career Change.
> Although designed with the BGSU audience in mind, if you're looking for
> possible careers and can't figure out what to do next, this Web site can
> give you some clues.

Mapping Your Future

http://mappingyourfuture.org/planyourcareer/

> The good people at Mapping Your Future can coach you through five
> steps in the career research and planning process: assessing your skills and
> interests, developing a career plan, researching careers, finding work, and
> reviewing other resources. Of particular interest on this site is CareerShip,
> an "online career exploration adventure" that is easy (and free) to use and
> powered by the Department of Labor's O*NET database.

What Can I Do With a Major In...

www.uncwil.edu/stuaff/career/Majors/index.htm

> Making the leap from school to work can be a big challenge, but help
> is available. What Can I Do With a Major In... provides a list of majors
> available at the University of North Carolina Wilmington (and most other
> universities). Pick any major to see a brief description, a list of careers that
> match that major, a list of related skills, links to Web sites that list job
> openings for those types of careers, career planning information, related
> organizations and associations, and miscellaneous resources.

Self-Assessment

You might have noticed that the first step in the sites just discussed generally is
self-assessment: the process of working to identify, understand, and express your
skills, knowledge, abilities, interests, values, personality, motivations, passions, and

anything else about you that might affect your career decisions. This makes sense. You need to figure out who you are and what you want before you can make an informed choice about your future (or next) career. But self-exploration can be a daunting task, so the Web sites in this section provide a variety of self-assessment tools to help you start this process, from validated tests administered by professionals to quizzes to writing or journaling exercises.

About Career Planning

http://careerplanning.about.com/od/selfassessment/

> About.com scores with this section specifically on career planning. In addition to links to online career assessments, you can read up on how self-assessments fit into your career planning process, which is also described here in a four-step process. Know the difference between a values inventory and a personality inventory? You will after you visit this site and maybe even take an assessment or two.

AdvisorTeam

www.advisorteam.com/temperament_sorter/register.asp

> Register for no fee and take the Keirsey Temperament Sorter II. This 70-question personality tool helps you discover your personality type, something that might be useful to know when making career decisions. Dr. David Keirsey's Temperament Theory sorts people into four temperament groups—artisans, guardians, rationals, and idealists—which are further sorted into 16 character types. You can read descriptions of the four temperament groups and their character types here. These character types tie directly to potential occupations of interest as well.

The Big Five Personality Test

www.outofservice.com/bigfive/

> UC Berkeley psychologist Frank J. Sulloway provides this 48-question test to measure "the five fundamental dimensions of personality." Its unique feature is that you are encouraged to answer each question both from your own perspective and as another person you know well. Your and the other person's percentile results (as compared to others who have taken this online test) are explained in five areas: Openness to Experience/Intellect, Conscientiousness, Extroversion, Agreeableness, and Neuroticism. You'll

also find links to other personality sites on the Web that let you learn more about the Big Five approach and your results. This site is also available in German, Spanish, and Dutch.

The Career Key

www.careerkey.org

If you want to invest in a professional-quality career test, check out The Career Key. Based on Holland's Theory of Career Choice, The Career Key meets professional-level standards of reliability and validity. In other words, it measures what it sets out to measure, and it does so consistently. Take the assessment online for $9.95 and read the articles on skills to better understand the theory. The Career Key is the work of Lawrence K. Jones, Ph.D., a professor emeritus from North Carolina State University and author of several career-related publications.

Enneagram Institute

www.enneagraminstitute.com

Learn about the Enneagram theory of nine personality types at this Web site by Don Richard Riso and Russ Hudson, two of the leading Enneagram teachers and developers. Take the sampler version of the Riso-Hudson Enneagram Type Indicator online to discover your type, or pay a fee for the full assessment and report. The site is a good source of other resources, including an active discussion board, books, and articles, for further exploration of this fascinating tool.

International Assessment Network: MAPP

www.assessment.com

Explore your career interests based on understanding what motivates you. MAPP stands for Motivational Appraisal of Personal Potential. Register for free to take a sample assessment intended to identify your motivations, interests, and talents. Your results and supporting material, including five job descriptions, are e-mailed to you. MAPP can produce a range of reports with additional information and assessments for a variety of fees. Sample reports and FAQs help you determine your individual needs. In addition, assessment.com offers other career-related tests that you can take for a fee.

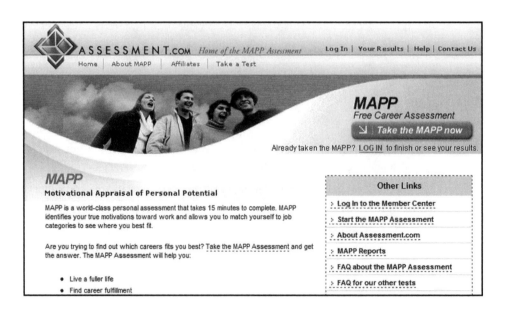

LiveCareer

www.livecareer.com

>According to the researchers at Live Career, there are more than 36,000 possible careers to choose from. This free assessment, developed by Dr. Douglas Jackson and taken by over a million people, can help you match your interests to careers. You can then use your personalized report to discover the experience, education, and training you need to make your next career move. The assessment is free with registration and takes approximately 25 minutes to complete.

O*NET Skills Search

http://online.onetcenter.org/skills/

>Studies have shown that choosing a career based on skills you have and enjoy is a sound approach to career development. The O*NET Skills Search is designed to help you use your skill set to identify occupations for exploration. You start by selecting a set of skills from six broad groups of skills and creating your customized skill list. One click produces a list of occupations that match your skills, and another click on any of the occupations gives you a detailed report of that occupation. Report topics include tasks, knowledge, skills, abilities, work activities, work context, work styles, work values, related occupations, wages and employment, and more.

The Personality Page

www.personalitypage.com/

> When you understand your personality, you may gain insight into what
> could make you happy in a career. Personality typing is based on the work
> of psychologist Carl Jung and, later, Isabel Briggs Meyers, who created the
> popular Myers-Briggs Type Indicator (MBTI). This site offers a 60-
> question personality questionnaire for a nominal fee that tells you which
> of 16 personality types you fit into. Alternatively, you can read about per-
> sonality typing—and there's plenty here to read—and then categorize your
> own behavior. If you're still foggy on your own type, consider investing in
> having a professional administer and interpret the full MBTI for you. For
> more information, visit the Center for Applications of Psychological Type
> at www.capt.org.

Queendom.com Career Tests

www.queendom.com/tests/career

> Are you suited for that IT job you're considering? Just for fun, find out
> by taking the IT Job Fit Test at Queendom.com. The site offers a large
> variety of tests (self-assessments, actually) in the areas of IQ, career, per-
> sonality, and health. The number of tests available depends on whether
> you register for a fee or for free. The no-fee offerings are fairly generous
> as well as interesting (why not try the Hairdresser Aptitude Assessment?),
> making a visit here worthwhile. Queendom.com's slogan is "Seriously
> entertaining."

Informational Interviewing

One of the best ways to learn more about the real-world aspects of a given career
is by talking to people currently working in the field. This section shows you how.

Information Interviews (Florida State University)

www.career.fsu.edu/experience/information-interviews-guide.html

> If ads at other sites distract you, get the plain facts here. This site is a nice
> summary overview of the informational interviewing process, including
> why to do one, who you should contact, where you can find these people,

and how you should prepare for your informational interview. You'll also find ideas on questions to ask, information on setting up the interview, pointers for handling the interview, and follow-up suggestions.

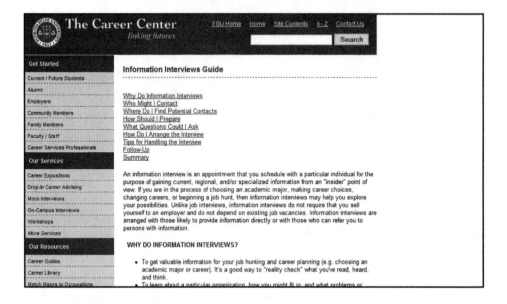

Informational Interview: About.com

http://jobsearch.about.com/od/infointerviews/Informational_Interviews.htm

This section from the Job Searching directory in About.com provides the basics on informational interviewing—what to do before, during, and after. See a sample letter to send to set up an informational interview, review a list of questions to choose from, find out how to evaluate what you learned from the interview, and learn to write a good thank-you letter. You'll find plenty of links to additional reading and resources as well.

Quintessential Careers: Informational Interviewing Tutorial

www.quintcareers.com/informational_interviewing.html

This tutorial walks you through the informational interview process, from identifying people to interview to doing your homework beforehand to evaluating the information you receive. The information is laid out in an easy-to-follow outline. You'll also find a ton of sample questions to spark your thoughts on what you might ask your contact.

U.S. Department of Labor Career Information

An educated, well-trained workforce is a key element of a healthy economy. The U.S. Department of Labor (DOL) is the leading federal agency for employment-related programs and statistics. It shares its research and information with all job seekers through several comprehensive Web sites.

America's Career InfoNet

www.acinet.org/acinet/

America's Career InfoNet (ACINet) is part of the CareerOneStop suite of Web sites from the U.S. Department of Labor (see America's Job Bank and America's Service Locator in chapter 4). At this site, you'll find national, state, and local career information and labor market data using career reports, videos, a career resource library, and other innovative Web-based tools. Under Occupation Information, you can view occupation lists sorted by characteristics such as the fastest-growing or the most openings, or compare wages and trends. You can also build a profile of an occupation, choosing only the attributes you're most interested in. Industry Information lists the fastest-growing industries, those with the largest employment, and declining industries. State Information provides you with demographic, employment, and services data and links to state labor market information. ACINet also offers a series of interactive career tools for career, education, and business decisions.

BLS Career Information

www.bls.gov/k12/index.htm

Designed with high school students in mind, this site provides an easy-to-use system for career exploration. Starting with the question "What do you like?" you can explore careers that are related to your interests, leading to brief descriptions of the career, what you need to do to prepare for it, and a list of related jobs. This site is a good starting point for young career explorers, although you will want to use the provided links to the *Occupational Outlook Handbook* to get more detailed job descriptions once you've found one you are interested in.

Career Guide to Industries

www.bls.gov/oco/cg/

> The Career Guide to Industries from the Bureau of Labor Statistics allows you to locate career information by industry. Just select a broad category from the links on the right, or choose the A–Z Index to search for a particular industry by name. Information on each includes the nature of the industry, working conditions, employment, occupations in the industry, training and advancement, outlook, earnings, and lists of organizations that can provide additional information. You might want to start with the "How Industries Differ" page for an overview of how understanding current industry conditions can help you find the job outlook and employment conditions for each. This is a companion guide to the *Occupational Outlook Handbook* (discussed in a moment).

Career Voyages

www.careervoyages.gov

> Whether you're a student, career changer, parent of a young adult, or career advisor, you'll find helpful career information here. Career Voyages is a collaboration of the U.S. Department of Labor and U.S. Department of Education. It's designed to provide information on high-growth, high-demand occupations, along with the skills and education needed to attain those jobs. After you read an industry profile, you can find information on the hiring outlook and wages for in-demand careers and view career videos online. Or you can explore the "hot careers" by state, by those requiring a four-year degree, or by those requiring less than a four-year degree. The Career Compass helps you learn more about using your interests as a guide to career selection.

Certification Finder

www.acinet.org/acinet/certifications_new/default.aspx

> A certification is evidence that you have knowledge, experience, or skills
> in an occupation or profession, usually proven by successfully passing
> an exam and/or series of classes. This handy site from America's Career
> InfoNet lets you search for certifications by keyword, industry, or occupa-
> tion. It lists certification and training providers alphabetically, with links
> to more information. Read the FAQs under Certification Finder Help for
> general information on certifications.

Licensed Occupations

www.careerinfonet.org/acinet/licensedoccupations/lois_state.asp

> To work as a hunting and fishing guide in some states, you need a license.
> In others, you don't. How can you know? For starters, visit Licensed
> Occupations, part of America's CareerInfoNet Workforce Credentials
> Information Center. At this site you can search the database of licensed
> occupations by occupation, agency, or keyword, and locate the contact
> information for the state licensing agency. Get all the FAQs on licensed
> occupations in the Help section.

Occupational Outlook Handbook

www.bls.gov/oco/

Every two years, the Bureau of Labor Statistics produces the *Occupational Outlook Handbook*—the best-known and most comprehensive book on occupations. The online version contains the same information as the printed copy, without the illustrations. The best way to find details on a particular occupation is to search by job title. Each description provides extensive information on the nature of the work, working conditions, training and education needed, advancement potential, employment statistics, job outlook, earnings, links to related occupations, and sources of additional information. You can read online or download a printer-friendly version of each report. Don't have a specific title in mind? Browse by broad category (construction, professional, armed forces, and so on) to access a list of job titles, and then read about those that interest you.

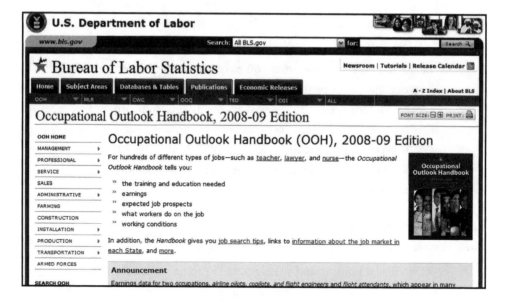

O*NET OnLine

http://online.onetcenter.org

O*NET, the Occupational Information Network, contains comprehensive job descriptions, including tasks; required knowledge, skills, and abilities; work activities and content; wages and employment; and more. Search for occupations by keyword, classification code, or field, or browse by O*NET descriptors. You can also use the skills checklists to find occupations that use your existing skills or search by job zones (essentially the level of education and training required to qualify for a particular job). After you look up an occupation, you can read a brief description, request further details, or search for related jobs to get ideas on other directions in which to take your career. Because O*NET is intended to provide standardized information to job seekers and employers, each description uses the same format and includes the same types of information, making it easy to compare potential career choices.

State-Based Career Information

Almost every state has a state-based career information system that contains searchable descriptions of occupations, programs of study, state and national colleges, private vocational schools, financial aid, scholarships, and more. The term "state-based" means that these state programs typically update the information annually and include salary ranges and hiring outlooks for occupations within that state. Because this data can and does vary in different areas of the country, the information in state-based systems is more detailed than similar nationwide data.

State-based career information system software programs are found in elementary schools, middle schools, and high schools; colleges and universities; job-training program sites; state workforce development sites; libraries; and other agencies serving the public.

Association of Computer-Based Systems for Career Information (ACSCI)
www.acsci.org/

Link to the state-based career information system in your state through the Association of Computer-Based Systems for Career Information (ACSCI) Web site. Visit the Web site or contact the state staff to learn how you can access the system. ACSCI also promotes standards of quality for career information—good to know if you're using the information for career decisions.

State Sources

www.bls.gov/oco/oco20024.htm

> This specific site, pulled from the online version of the *Occupational Outlook Handbook*, provides direct links to individual state career information delivery systems (CIDS). Find your state and follow the link to discover career and labor information including job outlook statistics, training information, and employment services.

Career Advice

There's no shortage of career advice to be found on the Internet. Many of the sites already listed contain articles, blogs, FAQs, and links to resources full of tips and pointers for advancing your career. Such sites hand out that advice as an added feature. The following sites make getting career advice the primary reason for visiting. Although you might find much of this same information elsewhere, it doesn't hurt to explore what other people are saying. It's your career, after all.

Brazen Careerist

www.brazencareerist.com

> The Brazen Careerists are a new generation of job seekers who aren't content with the traditional, cubicled, climb-the-corporate ladder mentality. Rather than play by the rules, they seek to create their own, fashioning career paths based on their personal interests and ambitions. By joining, you become part of one of the largest networks of young professionals, all willing to share their advice and experiences with fellow careerists. Read the blogs, contribute to the forums, offer your own advice, and research profiles of companies who cater to Generation Y workers. If you have a specific question or issue you need addressed, click on Coachology to have one of Brazen Careerist's career coaches respond (note that your identity remains anonymous).

Career Encouragement Blog

http://careerencouragement.typepad.com/the_career_encouragement_/

Even if you have all of the information (or think you do), sometimes you still need a little inspiration. The Career Encouragement Blog provides a daily dose of advice from a career coach and HR professional who has been in the business for 20 years. Blog topics are neatly organized by category and include topics you'd expect—such as Job Seeker Strategies and Starting a Business—and others that are designed to pick you up and push you along, such as Encouraging Quotes and Re-energize Your Career. The advice on this site isn't just for job seekers, but is geared toward anyone managing their career. It's as much about keeping and moving up in a job as it is getting one. You can comment on the articles, search the archives, or check out links to some useful resources as well.

Career Hub

www.careerhub.com

Career Hub is where the career experts come together and offer the same advice for free that they would charge for elsewhere. Here you can get most of your career and job search–related questions answered by experts in the field of career coaching. Research topics by category—from interviewing and resume writing to personal branding and online career marketing—or use the search feature to find something specific. Check out the long list of career blogs, download free e-books, or sign up for free updates. Rest assured, the advice you get here will be worth your time.

Career Management Alliance Blog

www.careermanagementalliance.com/blog/

If the Career Management Alliance sounds like a formidable group, there's good reason. This blog represents a collection of career news, trends, and tips from some of the leading career experts in the world. Entries are organized by category, with topics ranging the gamut from beginning job search to career advancement. You'll find tons of information on hot topics such as personal branding, social networking, managing your online identity, and more. Most importantly, you know the advice you're getting comes from people in the know—professionals who do this for a living. If you can't remember to visit the site, you can always subscribe to read the latest blogs by e-mail or RSS feed.

Lindsey Pollak Blog

http://lindseypollak.com/blog/

Career blogs are an excellent source of information, but much of it is general, aiming to appeal to as large an audience as possible. Not so with author and professional speaker Lindsey Pollak's blog, which caters directly to Generation Y. Nearly all of the articles and advice you'll find here is geared toward college students and young professionals just entering the workforce. As such, it tends to be timely, focused, and even a little hip. From this blog you can access a monthly podcast, peruse the author's list of recommended resources, subscribe to have the blog delivered to your e-mail, and read past published articles. Though it's not for everyone, this blog will appeal to young job seekers and recent graduates who don't want to read blogs about baby boomers looking to stretch their careers past retirement.

Secrets of the Job Hunt

www.secretsofthejobhunt.com/

This site pitches itself simply as "a social network for job seekers and career advice professionals," although it's actually an eclectic mix of career-related tools and information. Of course you are encouraged to become a member, to peruse and contribute to the forums and blogs, and to keep up to date on the latest career news. But you can also download podcasts, including interviews with leading professionals in career development, or listen to JobRadio.fm. One of the more interesting and informative tools is "Jobs in Pods," podcasts of career professionals discussing their jobs and answering questions about what the work is like. If your eyes cross looking at too much text on screen, the audio and video-intensive resources at this site might be a welcome, and informative, break.

Shifting Careers

http://shiftingcareers.blogs.nytimes.com/

The *New York Times* is one of the most well-respected news sources in the world, so it comes as no surprise that its career-related blog is also a good source for timely, professional advice. There aren't a lot of features here, so your best bet is to peruse the Tag List or to use the search tool to find posts on subjects that interest you. As of December 2008, this column was discontinued in the *New York Times*. But you can get future advice from writer Marci Alboher at http://heymarci.com.

Career Information Potpourri

You can find a mix of career exploration information from a variety of sources: professional associations, online newspapers and magazines, publishers, agencies, and more.

AARP: Careers

www.aarp.org/money/careers

Workers over the age of 45 make up 37 percent of the workforce, according to the U.S. Census Bureau. And the percentage of employees over the age of 65 is higher now than in the past 20 years. With more than 35 million members, AARP is the leading nonprofit, nonpartisan membership organization for Americans age 50 and over. This section of the AARP Web site covers choosing a career, job loss help, self-employment, and workplace flexibility with articles geared toward its members. In addition to basic career and job search information, find out about alternative work arrangements, discover clues that an employer welcomes older workers, learn about age-neutral employment practices, and get informed on how job accommodations can let you continue working even if you have a health condition or disability.

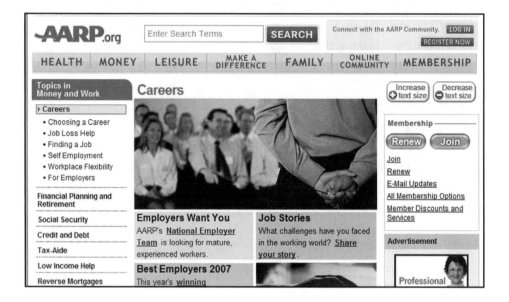

Barbara Sher

www.barbarasher.com

The outstanding feature on best-selling career author Barbara Sher's Web site are the extensive, active forums on a variety of subjects (listed under Bulletin Boards). Topics range from success stories to idea parties. Your questions can be answered by fellow members or by Sher herself. You'll also find ideas on starting your own "Success Team" with friends or finding a certified team leader near you. (Members of Success Teams support each other in achieving their dreams.)

Wall Street Journal: Career

http://online.wsj.com/public/page/news-career-jobs.html

This site is loaded with information on all aspects of careers, but this should come as no surprise, since it's from the *Wall Street Journal*. Salary information, job hunting advice, human resources issues, executive recruiting, college information—it's all here. Find daily feature career articles, search the database of free and low-cost events, join discussion boards, and read special reports. You can also add your resume to the database or sign up for customized e-mail job listings. Click the site map link to access all articles and resources by subject area.

Careers in Business

http://careers-in-business.jobsinthemoney.com/index.php

If you mean business about having a business career, check out this site. Careers in Business profiles careers in accounting, consulting, finance, marketing, and nonprofit management, providing information on skills, job options, salaries, trends, top firms, and recommended books on the subject. Search for jobs, post a resume, or subscribe to their newsletter for the latest information on business careers.

JIST Publishing

www.jist.com

JIST Publishing is your source for the best career, job search, business, and self-help books, videos, and software available today. This Web site delivers free career resources and weekly career-related tips, including Career Webinars recorded by experts in the field, and Best Jobs lists. Visit the site, browse the catalog online, request a free print catalog, and see for yourself. You can sign up for free e-mail newsletters, including "The Jist of It," which offers practical, self-directed information and articles that you can use in your work. You can also get caught up on breaking news in job search and careers by reading JIST's Job Search and Career Blog: http://jistjobsearchandcareer.blogspot.com/.

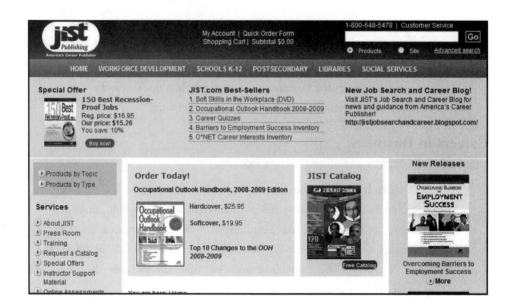

Job Accommodation Network (JAN)

www.jan.wvu.edu

> The purpose of JAN is to increase the employability of persons with dis-abilities. Through funding from the U.S. Department of Labor Office of Disability Employment Policy, JAN consultants work with people with disabilities and employers to create accommodation solutions that benefit and contribute to the hiring, retention, and promotion of this special-needs group. Services include toll-free consultations on employment, self-employment, and small-business options for persons with disabilities. The Web site contains more than 300 disability-specific publications, resources for purchasing accommodation equipment, and links to thousands of local, regional, national, public, and private resource organizations.

JobProfiles.org

www.jobprofiles.org

> For firsthand accounts from successful individuals in a variety of careers, visit JobProfiles.com. The profiles consist of questionnaires asking about the rewards, stress, basic skills, and challenges of jobs, as well as advice on entering the field. Organized by field of work, the profiles range from jobs in agriculture and nature to government and retail sales. Browse by category or search for profiles by keyword. Although one person's

perspective on a job or career may not be shared by everyone in that line of work, JobProfiles.com does provide a unique, insider's view of real-world work. This is recommended reading before you do informational interviews (as described earlier in this chapter).

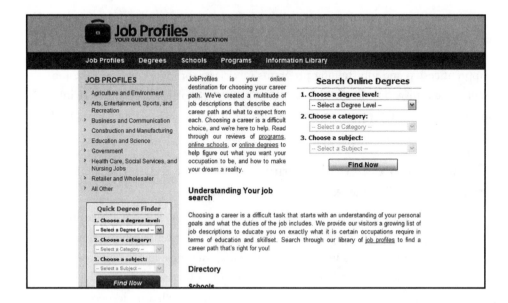

MyCareerBlast.com

www.mycareerblast.com

If you're on the verge of making the transition from school to the working world, this site is for you. At MyCareerBlast.com, you can get advice about choosing a college major or minor, uncover summer jobs and internships, get help with grad school decisions, read articles about achieving success on your first job, and find resources about freelancing or starting a business. All this is in addition to searching for a job and posting your resume.

Pam Pohly's Net Guide

www.pohly.com/index.html

If you're interested in a career in healthcare, you will want to bookmark this site. Pam Pohly Associates is a national management consulting firm with exclusive specialization in healthcare. Here you will find loads of resources covering all aspects of the business of healthcare, from personnel management to a glossary of managed-healthcare terms. This site also has links and contact information for state and regional hospital associations, healthcare and medical professional associations, healthcare recruiters, healthcare companies and hospitals, professional journals, and much more.

Apprenticeships and Job Training

Apprenticeship and job training programs mix classroom work with on-the-job training and provide entry into high-skill, rewarding professions. For more information on these and other job training programs (in the U.S.), contact the workforce development office in your state.

Canadian Apprenticeship Forum

www.caf-fca.org/english/index.asp

The Canadian Apprenticeship Forum (CAF-FCA) is a not-for-profit organization that promotes and supports the apprenticeship training and education systems in Canada. In Canada, each province or territory is responsible for setting the rules and regulations for apprenticeship training, and a special "Red Seal" endorsement permits skilled tradespeople to work anywhere in Canada. Here you'll find links to each provincial/territorial governmental apprenticeship Web site, as well as FAQs for both apprentices and employers. This site is available in both English and French.

Job Corps

http://jobcorps.doleta.gov

Job Corps is a no-cost education and vocational training program administered by the U.S. Department of Labor that helps young people ages 16 to 24 get a better job, make more money, and take control of their lives. Find out about the program, eligibility requirements, and interview process online, download the Job Corps information brochure, and then call the 800 number to get your questions answered and be referred to a local admissions counselor. If you've already gone through the program, you can join the National Job Corps Alumni Association.

Registered Apprenticeship

www.doleta.gov/OA/eta_default.cfm

> This site from the U.S. Department of Labor serves both individuals look-
> ing for apprenticeships and employers seeking to set up apprenticeship
> programs. This is your source of general information about apprentice-
> ship programs in the U.S. as well as links to places to find a program.
> Apprenticeships teach a trade through a combination of on-the-job train-
> ing and related instruction. They can be one of the best ways to learn the
> ins and outs of a particular occupation.

Salary Information

Use the sites in this section to learn the average pay rates in your chosen field, get
tips on salary negotiation, and find cost-of-living information for different parts of
the country.

JobStar: Salary Info Index

http://jobstar.org/tools/salary/

> Although this site also has career guides and resume information, JobStar is
> best known for its salary information. It's tempting to jump directly
> to JobStar's more than 300 links to general and profession-specific salary

surveys, but take some time to explore salary-negotiation strategies and test your own salary IQ first. Information on print resources you might want to check out is also included.

Quintessential Careers: Salary-Negotiation Tools

www.quintcareers.com/salary_negotiation.html

Don't get intimidated at the thought of negotiating a salary—get educated! Quintessential Careers offers a salary-negotiation tutorial for starters and a salary negotiation, compensation, and job offer quiz to test your skills. Learn how to write a counterproposal to bump up that job offer, see suggestions for dealing with salary history requests, and learn the basic do's and don'ts of salary negotiations. Anyone can negotiate a salary. Some time invested here can pay big dividends down the road of your career.

Salary.com

www.salary.com/

This site's name speaks to its focus, but it doesn't encompass all the site has to offer. Of course the site's primary goal is to help employers and employees better understand and meet each other's compensation needs, and the site itself is broken down into Personal, Small Business, and Enterprise sections—with different tools, programs, and resources for each. The personal side offers the Salary Wizard, an in-depth salary-calculation program that will produce a personal salary report. It even has separate "wizards" for mom and dad, one that helps you account for cost-of-living differences, a benefits calculator, and a college tuition planner. It also has a variety of job search tools, including a Job Search Wizard (to find openings), a college degree program finder, and advice on job performance, personal finance, relocation, and online learning. It's much more than a salary calculator, but you can be sure that it's probably got one of the best one of those as well. Registration is free, but be careful what you sign up for as some extras might cost you.

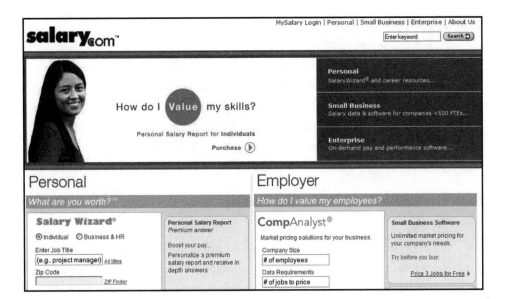

The Salary Calculator

www.homefair.com/real-estate/salary-calculator.asp

> Thinking about relocating for a job? Compare the cost of living among
> hundreds of U.S. and international cities with this handy salary calculator
> from HomeFair.com. Just enter your salary and current location, and then
> select another city to find out what you'll need to make there to sustain
> the same standard of living. While here, check out other relocation tools
> as well.

Salary Expert

www.salaryexpert.com

> Find free regional salary reports by selecting your job title and then your
> ZIP code or city. Reports list the position's average salary, benefits, and
> bonuses; show how salaries in a given area compare to the national aver-
> age; provide a brief description of the occupation; give the average cost of
> living in the area; and list links to salary information for related jobs. Also
> available here are selected feature articles and international salary reports.

Benefits

Most of us work for more than a paycheck. A compensation package ideally includes benefits such as health insurance, paid time off, retirement, savings programs, and a variety of other offerings. Benefits vary widely from organization to organization, and employers use a good benefits package as a hiring incentive. Understanding what benefits are, and appreciating their value to you, can help you identify employers you'd like to work for.

Employee Benefit Research Institute

www.ebri.org/

> For 30 years, the Employee Benefit Research Institute has been the only nonprofit, nonpartisan organization focused on researching and educating people about employee benefits. Its site offers a comprehensive—if not exactly easy-to-navigate—look at current trends in employee compensation. Your best bet is to start with the resources section. Check out What's New in Employee Benefits, peruse Special Issues of Periodicals focused on benefits, or just look over the Benefit FAQ for straightforward overviews of the concerns most workers have regarding their retirement, health insurance, taxes, and other benefit-related issues.

Job Loss Strategies

Layoffs occur for a host of reasons: automation, bankruptcy, a business ownership change, contracts completed or canceled, foreign competition, natural disasters, and more. When you hear about them in the news, it's merely news. When you're caught in the middle, it's your livelihood. But, as these sites point out, this doesn't have to be cause for despair.

Career OneStop

www.servicelocator.org/

> If you've lost your job, one of the first steps you should take is to visit your local One-Stop Career Center. Professionals there can help you apply for unemployment benefits, find your next job, get additional education or training, explore alternative careers, update your resume, and much more.

Of course, to make a visit, you have to know where you are going. With America's Service Locator you can easily find the One-Stop Center nearest you simply by typing your ZIP code. You will be presented with a list of nearby options; clicking any of them leads you to detailed information about the services that office offers, as well as details for how best to contact them.

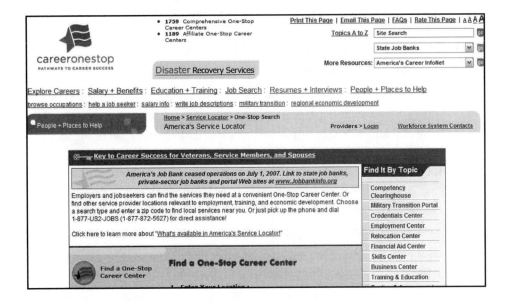

Fast Company: 10 Hard Truths About Layoffs

www.fastcompany.com/articles/2001/06/10truths.html?page=0%2C1

The truth is…that the truth is hard to handle. Still, finding your next job will be easier if you know what you are getting into. Visit this site to learn the 10 Hard Truths About Layoffs. There you will learn that your unemployment might last longer than expected, that you might have to take a lower salary than you are used to, and that you might have to move to a different city to jump-start your career. While the article is sobering, it can at least help you identify possible barriers you will face to employment, which in turn will help you overcome them.

State Unemployment Benefits Offices Locator

www.servicelocator.org/OWSLinks.asp

> While the home page of America's Service Locator will help you find Career One-Stops, which in turn offer a broad range of services, this site focuses on unemployment benefits. Click on the state where you work for direct links to offices and resources to help you file for these benefits. Sometimes you can even file directly over the Internet.

What To Do If You're Being Laid Off

www.investsafe.com/development/advice.html

> The answer: Go to this Web site and read through the 39 tips for coping with job loss. A little preparation and smart thinking can go a long way toward easing the pain of job loss and speeding up the regrouping and transition process. It's good to know where to look for practical advice if and when you need it.

When the Paycheck Stops

www.aflcio.org/issues/jobseconomy/unemployment/handbook/index.cfm

> This unemployment resource booklet, created and hosted by the AFL-CIO, contains useful information on how to survive job loss. Topics include finding help, managing your finances, staying healthy, and getting another job. The AFL-CIO Web site offers other resources for the unemployed, including an unemployment checklist, information on worker's compensation, and links to other Web sites.

CHAPTER 4

Finding and Applying for Job Openings

One thing is for sure—the Internet has no shortage of job information. In the early days of the Internet, employment professionals and recruiters saw the Internet's tremendous potential, with its ability to reach millions of people, and they jumped on with enthusiasm. Over the years, three trends have emerged: General job bank sites have gotten bigger and have become more sophisticated with search capabilities, the number of specialty job banks is growing, and almost all of the sites now want you to register, either for free or for a fee.

Typical features on these sites include the ability to search and apply for jobs, post your resume for employers to view, and be notified of openings that match criteria you establish. Job banks usually charge employers and recruiters to post positions. Some sites, called aggregators, pull openings together from multiple job sites to provide a more comprehensive list. Most sites allow you to search their listings but require you to register before you can apply.

Registering means different things on different sites. Some sites only ask you for a valid e-mail address and password. Others request more extensive information, using it to compile a demographic profile of their customers and to elicit more business from employers and advertisers. The sites or their affiliates might also send you advertising. Look for a privacy policy regarding the use of your personal information, which should also clarify your opt-out options. If privacy is an issue for you, use only a job bank whose policies you understand and accept.

Speaking of advertising, be forewarned—the noncommercial job bank has become something of a rarity. A pop-up blocker can eliminate the most annoying ads. If action ads distract you, you can probably find a site without them. In addition to visual ads, several sites promote fee-based job search services such as resume writing and job coaching.

Consider limiting the number of job bank sites you use. With all you have to choose from, you can be selective. Try searching for the same job or job type in several job banks, and evaluate the results. How current is the information? Are posting dates listed? Do the positions come directly from employers, or are they from recruiters? Does the site provide good contact information on the companies, with links to their Web sites? After thoroughly evaluating several sites, you will decide on your favorites. Happy job hunting!

Government Sources of Job Information

Let's start with the Internet resources that are funded with your tax dollars. Both state and federal governments sponsor employment-related Internet sites that can link you to a number of job listings. (For information on jobs with the government itself, see the listings in the section "Other Specialized Job Banks" later in this chapter.)

U.S. Department of Labor

America's Service Locator
www.servicelocator.org

With the disappearance of America's Job Bank (the national job bank compiled by the federal government), the focus shifts to state and local resources to find jobs. Find the local workforce services you need through America's Service Locator. One-stop career centers, located in every state, provide convenient services to workers and employers, such as information on job training programs, unemployment insurance, education opportunities, career services, and more. Search for the center nearest you by city or ZIP code and get the address, complete with driving instructions and a map. For handy, up-to-date links to your state's workforce-related Web sites, see the state Web directory. Alternatively, you can go to www. jobbankinfo.org to link directly to your state's own job bank (you only need to find it on a map). America's Service Locator is part of the DOL's CareerOneStop toolkit (see America's Career InfoNet, described in chapter 3).

General Job Banks

General Internet job banks draw from different sources and present their job postings in different ways. Visit several to see what we mean and find the ones you like the best.

BestJobsUSA.com

www.bestjobsusa.com

BestJobsUSA monitors over 300 major newspapers' employment sections each day. Try the state site selection option, which includes a separate jobs page focused on each U.S. state. On each of these pages, you can conduct a job search in only that state and find local articles and information. Registered job seekers have the option of posting and managing their resumes online, with an optional masking option to hide personal and contact information. Also check out the virtual career fairs, corporate profiles, and various lists of top employers.

CareerBuilder.com

www.careerbuilder.com

Search the classifieds of over 150 newspapers at this one handy site. CareerBuilder.com lets you sort by keyword, city, state, field of interest, company, industry, or job type. Use their job-matching technology to have jobs openings e-mailed to your inbox. You also can post your resume online (at your choice of three different privacy levels). Take career assessments, get career advice, and have your resume critiqued. Free registration entitles you to additional services such as job search management and resume posting tools.

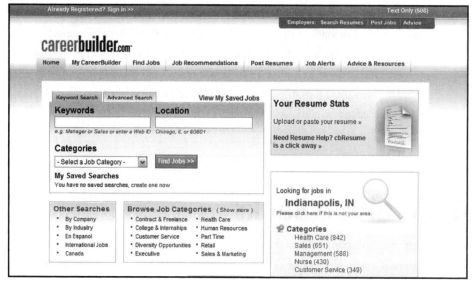

Craigslist

www.craigslist.org

It may not be much to look at, but there is no doubting the sheer volume of information that Craigslist provides. Essentially a giant collection of classifieds, Craigslist posts over 30 million new advertisements each month, at least two million of them job listings. Although that is a tremendous amount to sift through, the process is straightforward: just find your city (or the closest one to where you live) and find the category you are looking for (jobs, presumably, although you might also be on the lookout for a used car or a hot date). From there it's just like looking through the classifieds section of your Sunday newspaper—if your Sunday newspaper served 50 countries worldwide and was a million pages long.

jobfox

www.jobfox.com

Jobfox takes a more personalized approach to the job bank formula by providing you with "introductions" to companies and vice versa. You start by creating a profile using jobfox's mini-interview approach. They then use their Mutual Suitability System to match your experience, skills, and interests with companies' needs, giving you a selective list of job openings tailored to you. Rather than simply provide you with a list of openings, jobfox uses e-mail and sometimes direct telephone contact to introduce you and the company to each other. You can even create your own Web page to highlight your skills and experience. Jobfox was founded by Rob McGovern, also the founder and former Chairman and CEO of CareerBuilder.com (discussed previously).

Monster

www.monster.com

Monster, possibly the best-known career site on the Internet, contains all the features you'd expect from a major job and resume bank. Get tips on getting the most out of the site by visiting the Career Advice section. Your options here include registering to post your resume, having jobs e-mailed to you, signing up for e-mail newsletters, searching more than one million monthly job postings, and applying online using your posted resume. You'll also find advice, articles, discussion boards, and tools in an extensive online career center. Monster also offers additional services for a fee, such as resume writing assistance and career coaching. You can get the most up-to-date information and tips by subscribing to the Monster blog: http://monster.typepad.com/monsterblog/.

NationJob

www.nationjob.com

Search for jobs or sign up to have P.J. Scout do it for you. Just tell him exactly what you want, and whenever he finds a job opening of interest to you, he will e-mail you a detailed job description, including "how to apply" information. All you need is an e-mail address. Read job seeker success stories, browse company profiles, and even subscribe for free to trade magazines.

RealMatch

www.realmatch.com

Like jobfox (see above), RealMatch uses specialized software to directly match job candidates to employers. Both employers and job seekers specifically define themselves, their needs, and their preferences. RealMatch then fits the pieces together so that your information is only provided to companies that could really use your skills and companies contact you only if you are interested. You can do all of this for free and anonymously, so that a current employer doesn't accidentally happen upon your profile. With a million potential job matches available, it's definitely worth a try.

snagajob.com

www.snagajob.com

Billed as the "#1 source for hourly and part-time jobs," snagajob posts more than 100,000 job listings from employers across the country. Search for jobs by ZIP code or create a profile and have openings e-mailed to you. This site also includes practical advice for students, teens, moms, and others who would be interested in part-time or seasonal employment.

Vault.com

www.vault.com

Vault is known for its insider information on more than 5,000 companies and 70 industries. Vault's Electronic Watercooler (under "Message Boards") is the Internet's first collection of company-specific message boards for employees, where anyone can network, ask for job advice, or learn what it's like to work for a certain company. In addition, Vault offers one of the most extensive collections of online career reference resources, including sample cover letters, resumes, and interview questions, and video guides. More information is available for a fee. All of this is in addition to the job bank itself and resume posting and matching services—much of it focused on helping individuals find and land high-paying, high-growth jobs.

Yahoo! HotJobs

http://hotjobs.yahoo.com

> Use the advanced search feature at HotJobs to refine your results list.
> Under Advanced Job Search, you can search by keyword, up to three
> job categories or two locations, level of experience, and minimum salary.
> You can also screen out jobs posted by staffing firms if you want to deal
> directly with employers rather than applying through agencies. You must
> log in to post a resume or save your search results, but if you already have
> a Yahoo! e-mail account, it's your same username and password. While
> you're searching for jobs, use Yahoo!'s Career Tools to polish your resume
> or cover letter or prep for your next interview.

Job Board Aggregators

Aggregators are essentially giant search engines that pull information from multiple
sources. In the case of job boards, these aggregators filter the results from all of
the major job sites (such as Monster and CareerBuilder), as well as newspapers and
corporate job boards. The result is a more comprehensive approach to job searching—essentially the aggregator has gone and visited hundreds of Web sites for you.
Although these aggregator sites may produce more job openings, they tend to have
fewer other career resources and tools than other job banks.

Indeed

www.indeed.com

> Indeed.com includes all the job listings from major job boards, newspa-
> pers, associations, and company HR pages. You can search by keyword or
> location or use the advanced search to limit results by type of job, salary
> range, date posted, or the source of the listing itself. You can save your
> searches or have the results delivered to you using your e-mail or one of
> many RSS readers.

Jobster

www.jobster.com

> Jobster is an efficient, streamlined aggregator that's easy to use and elegant
> in its simplicity. Search for jobs by category, job title, or ZIP code; or

use the advanced search to narrow down by posting date, location, and Boolean parameters. You can also upload your resume and create a profile so that employers registered with Jobster can find you or register to have job alerts sent to your e-mail. No career advice, no blogs, no distractions—for people who just want to know what's out there.

Simply Hired

www.simplyhired.com

This award-winning site aims to make online job searching simple, effective, and enjoyable. You can search by keyword, location, job category, industry, or company. You can filter results by job type, requirements, education, date, and even by company size and revenue. Create a profile and post your resume so that you can respond to listings directly. You can rate each job result and eventually SimplyHired.com will begin suggesting job listings based on those ratings. You can also use its salary calculator or check out job trends nationally or locally.

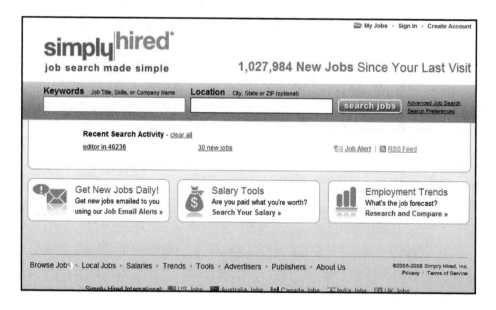

Job Banks for Recent or Soon-to-Be College Graduates

The sites in this section represent a large variety of work opportunities and career advice targeted at college students and recent graduates. If you're new to the workforce, you might find your ideal entry-level job here more easily than you would at a larger job bank.

AfterCollege

www.aftercollege.com

> Search among the more than 150,000 entry-level jobs from over 30,000 employers. AfterCollege also has listings of internships, guides for working abroad, and job channels to help you focus your search. And don't forget the resume-posting service, which converts any resume written in most common word processing programs.

The Black Collegian Online

www.blackcollegian.com/

> This award-winning site is the cyberspace partner of *The Black Collegian* magazine, serving the career and self-development interests of African-American college students since 1970. This site has plenty of career planning and job search information, as well as lifestyle/entertainment features and college life news. Post your resume or review job openings with equal-opportunity employers.

CBcampus.com

www.careerbuildercollege.com

> CBcampus.com is a division of CareerBuilder, the nation's largest job site. Here college students, recent graduates, and alumni can find job opportunities suited to their major and current experience level. You can search for both jobs and internships by keyword, company, location, or category. You can also post and manage your resume or have it reviewed by CareerBuilder staff. While you're visiting, sign up for job alerts, check out career fairs in your area, peruse the job and internship blog, and get advice on all aspects of the job search. It's the power of CareerBuilder focused on the needs and prospects of the college graduate.

CollegeGrad.com

www.collegegrad.com

> CollegeGrad.com is devoted to entry-level job information. It contains extensive resources for new graduates seeking to enter the job market. Sections include career planning, resumes, cover letters, employer research, job postings, interviewing, salaries, and your new job. The job search section is broken into entry-level, internships, and experience-required categories, helping you zero in on your best opportunities.

CollegeRecruiter.com

www.collegerecruiter.com

> Conduct a traditional job search, or browse openings by career channel. Free membership allows you to post your resume and have job notices e-mailed to you. In addition, check the Advice and Resources link for a nice collection of industry information, including hiring prospects, the most common personality types for specific occupations, and career videos. Free industry magazines, blogs, podcasts, and even a couple of games are here as well.

Get That Gig

www.getthatgig.com

> As the name suggests, Get That Gig targets members of the younger generation, particularly their desire for jobs outside of the standard, office, nine-to-five. This isn't to say that you won't find those traditional job listings here, only that the site doesn't emphasize them, instead focusing on "cool people in cool jobs." Search by category (including Music, Entertainment, and Art & Design) to find links to both jobs and internships. What the site lacks in overall features—you won't find much in the way of career advice or job search tools here—it makes up for in pizzazz.

InternJobs.com

www.internjobs.com

> InternJobs.com is a global database of internships for students, recent graduates, and career changers. Search by location, keyword, or top jobs. Postings are generous in the information they provide. They include complete information on the hiring organization, including a link to the company Web site for further investigation.

JobWeb

www.jobweb.com

> You won't find specific job openings at JobWeb, but you will find an extensive, searchable database of employers looking for career-minded graduates. Sponsored by the National Association of Colleges and Employers, JobWeb's primary audience is recent or soon-to-be college graduates. Other sections include resume and interview advice and a large library of career-related articles and career-planning information.

MonsterTRAK

www.monstertrak.com

> MonsterTRAK, a division of Monster, offers college students and recent graduates a variety of services, including searching for that first job or internship. Get career advice and networking opportunities from alums at your own school, research companies, participate in message boards and chats, find resume advice, and browse an online career fair. You'll also find career-related articles and tools, as well as a whole new section on finding and landing a "green" career.

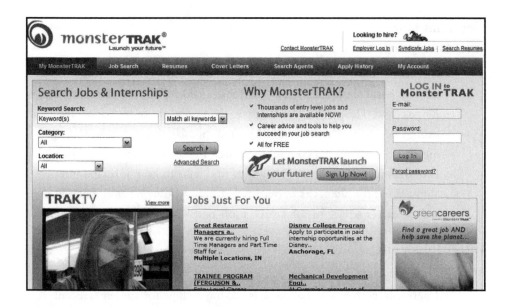

Other Specialized Job Banks

Specialized job banks aimed at specific groups or targeted to a particular field are one of the best ways to zero in on appropriate listings and cut through the clutter of crowded general databases. This section contains a sampling of the resources available. You can find more by browsing the clearinghouses described later in this chapter or by conducting an online search, as explained in the Introduction to this book.

911hotjobs.com
http://911hotjobs.com

If careers in law enforcement or firefighting sound exciting, call on 911hotjobs.com. Search free job listings, or sign up as a paid member to search jobs from 911hotjobs.com together with those from other law enforcement Web sites. The membership fee is charged monthly to your credit card, and you can cancel at any time. You can also order law enforcement employment and examination preparation books, sign up for a newsletter that notifies you when new positions are posted, or, for a fee, take online practice tests.

Absolutely Health Care

www.healthjobsusa.com

> The health care industry is the fastest-growing source of new jobs in the United States. It should come as no surprise, then, that this award-winning site lists more than 275,000 health care jobs throughout the country. You can browse jobs by keyword, category, job titles, city, state, or company. You can also post your resume and set up a job search agent (free of charge) in the hopes that an employer will find and contact you. Absolutely Health Care also includes licensing information and a health-care salary wizard. At the very least, with so many jobs to choose from and more openings each day, you'll know that your skills as a health care professional are needed.

Career Center: idealist.org

www.idealist.org/en/career/index.html

> For those who really want to make a difference, there's idealist.org. The main site offers all kinds of information about nonprofit organizations, volunteer opportunities, and community action. The preceding link takes you directly to the career center, listing more than 6,000 jobs as well as resources for job seekers interested in starting a nonprofit career.

CivilianJobs.com

www.civilianjobs.com/

> CivilianJobs.com is the largest firm specializing in placing military candidates into civilian careers. Through its auto-matching technology, ex-military can find jobs that match their skills and interests and employers can recruit qualified personnel that have been prescreened. Other services to job seekers include assessment tools; advice on career planning, resume writing, and interviewing; and information on job fairs and the GI Bill. Registration is free for job seekers, provided that you currently serve or have served in the military (it is the first question asked upon registration, and answering no won't get you very far).

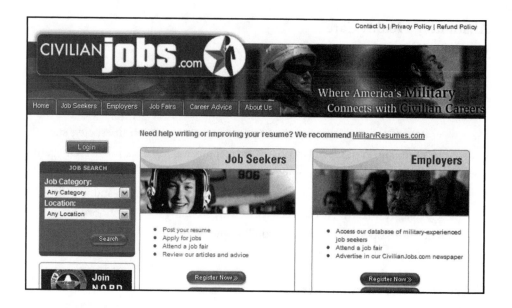

Cool Works

www.coolworks.com

> If ski resorts, dude ranches, national parks, and cruises sound like fun plac-
> es to work, get the scoop at the specialized job bank that is Cool Works.
> If you detect a note of enthusiasm for the types of jobs posted here, it
> may be because Cool Works is within shouting distance of Yellowstone
> National Park. Find the right adventure—internships, volunteer opportu-
> nities, guide jobs, conservation corps, and more—in addition to seasonal
> jobs. Visit the Get Started page under Job Seekers for helpful instructions
> on using the site. The Cool Works motto is "Thousands of jobs in great
> places."

CvTips.com

www.cvtips.com

> For job search information with an international flavor, visit this site by
> the University of Portsmouth, Great Britain. This no-frills site loaded with
> articles is aimed mainly at Brits, but if your dream job is abroad, informa-
> tion here may give you an edge and show you how to be a cosmopolitan
> job seeker.

dice.com

www.dice.com

Dice.com specializes in jobs for information technology (IT) professionals. Given the nature of the IT marketplace, a number of listings here are for contract positions rather than permanent opportunities. You can search the jobs by keyword, location, area code, type, and company. You can limit your search to telecommuting only or by the amount of travel required. You can also create a personalized account to have your profile available to employers (publicly or confidentially), create an online resume, join dice discussion boards, and use personal search agents.

govtjobs.com

www.govtjobs.com

Govtjobs.com matches applicants with state, county, and local government job listings. Check out the posted job opportunities organized by job categories. Govtjobs.com also has links to almost 150 national associations and federal agencies, as well as state-by-state resource information where you can go exploring for job opportunities. Better yet, no registration or membership is required to access the information.

Hard2Hire.org

www.hard2hire.org

Nearly one in four Americans has a significant hurdle to overcome in finding employment—a criminal record. Hard2Hire is a nonprofit 501.c.3 corporation dedicated to helping unemployed and underemployed people with criminal records get better jobs and improve their long-term economic prospects. Services for job seekers here include a jobs database matching service and personal improvement tools such as resume writing and interview skills.

JobsintheMoney

www.jobsinthemoney.com

> Don't let the name fool you: This isn't a Web site for finding jobs that
> will have you rolling *in* money (although most of them do pay well), but a
> site for finding careers working *with* money. JobsintheMoney.com, a Dice
> Holdings company, provides accounting and finance professionals with
> job opportunities, news, and advice specific to those industries. You can
> register for free, posting your resume so that companies can find you, or
> use the site's targeted job search to find openings in your field or area. All
> of the career news and advice is geared toward accounting and finance
> professionals, although much of it can be applied to the general job seeker
> as well. If you are looking to be an accountant or auditor, an investor or a
> CFO, this is a good place to start looking.

The Ladders

www.theladders.com/

> Granted the target audience might be limited, but if you are a job seeker
> used to making at least $100,000 a year, then The Ladders is the place
> to find your next high-paying gig. It provides job search and recruiting
> services to job seekers and companies in the areas of sales, marketing,
> finance, human resources, law, technology, and other $100k+ industries.

The site lists more than 35,000 new jobs per month (yes, there are 35,000 new jobs that pay at least a hundred grand), and provides unique networking opportunities between qualified applicants and companies on the lookout for top-tier talent. The Web site provides its basic job search service for free (provided that your most recent salary was $75,000 or more), although for as little as $30 per month you can upgrade your membership to take advantage of more networking and recruiting options. And even if you don't make that much a year, you can always hop over to the Career Advice section to find out what you can do start earning more and move up the ladder, as it were.

LatPro

www.latpro.com

LatPro claims to be the largest diversity employment Web site in the U.S. and the leading source for Spanish/English and Portuguese/English bilinguals throughout the Americas. A list of testimonials speaks highly of the site, which includes job search and resume posting features, career-related articles, e-mail newsletters, extensive information on immigration, and more. This site is available in English, Spanish, and Portuguese.

lawjobs.com

www.lawjobs.com

You don't have to have a law degree to work in a legal profession—attorneys make up only a portion of the industry's employees. Legal secretaries, paralegals, teachers, administrative and support personnel—they all have specialized skills and training to do their jobs. Here is a specialized site to help people interested in a legal career get those jobs. Like most specialized job banks, your search will be limited to those jobs in the profession (in this case, law), and you can search numerous ways. You can also find news and advice concerning legal careers, check out salary information, and browse directories of employers. New graduates can read the Student Recruitment Guide for information and articles about breaking into a legal profession. Of course, if you aren't interested in being a lawyer or helping lawyers, you are better off looking elsewhere.

Lisjobs.com

www.lisjobs.com

This site has lots of career information for librarians and information professionals, but what would you expect from information experts? Here you can search library job listings by keyword or browse by category or state. Other features on this site include articles and career advice on topics from interviewing to salaries, as well as a free professional development e-mail newsletter.

MarketingJobs.com

www.marketingjobs.com

Put your sales and marketing skills to work with MarketingJobs.com, a Web site focusing solely on positions in sales, marketing, and advertising. Search by keyword, job function, or state, or register and create an anonymous career profile and let employers find you. There aren't a lot of extras here, but if marketing is your career of choice, it's well worth the visit.

MedZilla

www.medzilla.com/

It may sound like the offspring of a Japanese monster movie menace, but MedZilla is actually the Web's premier job bank for medical, healthcare, and related professionals. Launched in 1994, it provides users with a search of more than 4,000 jobs in some of the economy's fastest-growing fields, from biotechnology to pharmaceuticals. Free registration allows you access to MedZilla's applicant-tracking and resume-management systems. You can also check out the site's career forums, research salary information, and read articles on job hunting in the medical profession.

Saludos.com

www.saludos.com

Saludos.com specializes in joining Hispanic bilingual professionals with companies looking for diversity in the workplace. Services for job seekers include listings of entry-level jobs and internships, a resume posting service, guides to researching specific fields, and additional career links. You'll also find online articles from *Saludos Hispanos* magazine.

School Spring

www.schoolspring.com

> Search for teaching jobs across the U.S. or create a free search agent and
> have positions e-mailed to you as they become available. You can custom-
> ize your search by location, job type, grade level, and job category; or you
> can search by keyword. School Spring also provides resources on certifica-
> tion, job fairs, and job search tips in education.

SeniorJobBank

www.seniorjobbank.org

> The workers of tomorrow are here today, and they have a ton of experi-
> ence. SeniorJobBank is aimed at the over-50 crowd, and anyone who is
> demographic-savvy knows that there are a lot of folks in this age group.
> In addition to industry, job category, and location, the search tool lets you
> choose the type of employment, ranging from short-term contract to full-
> time. Create up to three resumes with your free account with the option
> of allowing potential employers to view it, or have the personal job agent
> notify you of openings.

SummerJobs.com

www.summerjobs.com

Need to find summer or seasonal employment between semesters? SummerJobs.com is the place to start. Most of these ads come from camps, resorts, amusement parks, and other places that need seasonal help. You can also view employer profiles and links to their Web sites to find out about your potential summer employer. SummerJobs.com is part of the AboutJobs.com network.

Thingamajob Engineering

http://engineering.thingamajob.com/Browse-Jobs/

Thingamajob actually has separate job banks for a variety of technical industries and categories, including manufacturing, sales, automotive, and accounting. However the focus—and the lion's share—of its listings are in engineering. Owned and operated by Allegis, a staffing company that specializes in matching technical and administrative professionals with organizations in need, Thingamajob offers the typical menu of job bank options. You can search by subcategory, state, or province, and then follow the links to apply for jobs online (you will need to create a free account and post your resume first). Visit the Career Center for articles on career issues related to engineering and other technical professions, though be aware that the resources here are limited.

USAJOBS

www.usajobs.opm.gov

USAJOBS is the official site of the U.S. Office of Personnel Management. It's *the* place to go if you want to work for the federal government. The powerful search feature lets you sort current job openings by keyword, location, job category, salary range, federal pay grade, job series, agency, and more. To get started, you can view online job search and resume tutorials or download handy reference guides. The Information Center spells out everything you need to know and do to apply for a job, right down to completing the online resume. It also includes a Career Interests Center to help you assess your skills and interests and match them to potential federal opportunities.

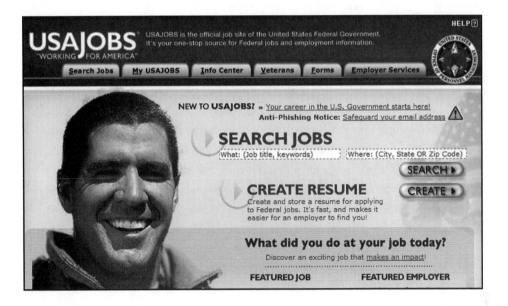

Regional Job Sites

If you're less than geographically mobile, or if you're interested in employment in a particular region, you might want to investigate job banks specializing in positions and career advice for specific large cities, states, or regions. This section contains a few examples.

California Jobs

www.californiajobs.com/

> California Jobs is one of many sites powered by LocalCareers.com. As you might expect, the site is first and foremost a job bank for opportunities in The Golden State, with the ability to browse by region, category, company, keyword, and job class. CaliforniaJobs.com offers numerous other tools for job seekers, including a continuing education guide, resources and articles, a free job-hunting guide, and a calendar of upcoming job fairs and events. Of special interest might be the information listed under relocation, which discusses how to engage in a long-distance job search and how to handle cost-of-living changes. After all, a $70,000 salary in San Francisco is barely enough to live on for most people.

ChicagoJobs.com

www.chicagojobs.com/

> The Windy City is home to two baseball teams, famous gangsters, and its own style of pizza. It is also a source of nearly every type of job imaginable (surf instructors not included). Most of the area's major newspapers come together on ChicagoJobs.com to match qualified applicants with open positions across all 11 Chicagoland counties. Register for free to have a job search agent find and e-mail you good matches, search for jobs by industry or category, and check out the salary information and career resources section. You can even watch video clips showcasing local job opportunities. If you aren't used to navigating these kinds of sites, this one provides its own User's Guide to help you get around.

FloridaJobs.com

www.floridajobs.com

> As the name suggests, FloridaJobs.com specializes in connecting Florida jobs and job seekers. After you register (for no cost), you can post a resume, with privacy options for how your information is used. You'll also find some tips and guidelines for taking full advantage of the site's offerings.

LocalJobBoard.com

www.localjobboard.com

> If you're unwilling or unable to relocate to find a job, try LocalJobBoard. com. All the jobs posted here are categorized by city, state, and industry, and some 5,464 cities have job postings. It's searchable, of course, and, as with most job banks, you can post your resume and create a job alert with a free membership. A nice extra is the local information—economy, employment, real estate, recreation, schools, and sports.

TriStateJobs.com

www.tristatejobs.com

> If you live in the Northeast, you might want to visit TriStateJobs.com for thousands of listings in New York, New Jersey, Connecticut, and Pennsylvania. You can search, post your resume, and sign up for e-mail notification of jobs matching your specifications. You also can check out information on local career fairs and find links to additional career sites and resources.

Jobing.com

www.jobing.com/

> With a plea to "join your local jobing community," Jobing.com runs several local job banks covering major cities in 19 states. With a free online account, you can build up to 10 resumes and cover letters; make your resume searchable, confidential, or hide it from individual employers; store and view the jobs for which you've applied; and create e-mail agents to notify you of openings.

Job Center of Wisconsin
https://jobcenterofwisconsin.com/

> Find your dream job in Wisconsin through its Job Center. Use its search engine to link up with the local job resources, such as area newspapers, state job center offices, public libraries, universities, and more, many of which have their own job listings. You can also find local labor market information or access other useful career resources.

Canadian Job Information

This section contains leads to jobs in Canada. For information on jobs in other countries, check the career clearinghouses listed later in this chapter, as well as Monster and other job banks previously described, several of which provide international listings or affiliate sites. Be aware, however, that many of these postings may be only for resident citizens.

Human Resources and Skills Development Canada: Job Bank
www.jobbank.gc.ca

> On any given day, Job Bank contains about 40,000 job postings across Canada, including a special section for student jobs. Pick your desired province, and then specify a job title or search by keyword to retrieve postings. Click on the "Working in Canada" link to find information on receiving an employment authorization if you are not a citizen or permanent resident. Job Bank also provides a number of links to other sites that are useful to Canadian job seekers. This site also is available in French.

Jobboom
www.jobboom.com

> At Jobboom, you can search for a specific job or an employer in Canada. Visit the Career Zone for information on career planning, dealing with workplace conflicts, and balancing your work and life. Registration is required to view some information and to apply for openings, but it's free, simple, and confidential. This site also is available in French.

Workopolis.com

www.workopolis.com

Search through more than 40,000 jobs in Canada, subscribe to a weekly JobMail newsletter, or take a tutorial in resume writing, networking, interviewing, or salary negotiation. Try the RSS (Really Simple Syndication) feature to have openings for job titles you select delivered to you in real time. Another handy feature is a direct link to the employer Web site for each posting for background research. Workopolis is a partnership of three Canadian media companies and appears in both English and French.

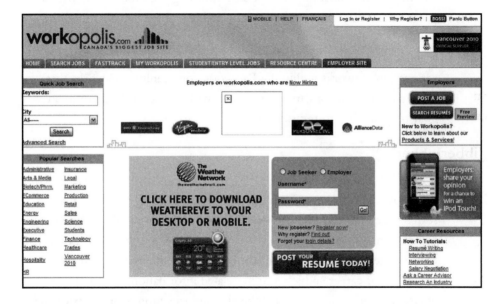

Online Networking

The last three years have witnessed an explosion in online networking, with sites like the ones listed here increasing their number of members at an exponential rate. You would be hard pressed to find a child of the digital age who doesn't have a Facebook or MySpace account. Although many networking sites are essentially social in nature (have a high school sweetheart you want to hook up with?), they also have immense value when it comes to finding a job or advancing your career. After all, networking is considered to be the best way to find work, and it's certainly the best way to stay aware of new opportunities. Online networking is essentially not that different from the offline version, except you chat on boards as opposed to over lunch. Just be aware that each of the following sites will ask you to set up an account, creating, in essence, an online version of you. Almost anything you put up there can, and often will, be accessed by potential employers. Keep your information professional, and don't say anything that might get you into trouble later.

Facebook
www.facebook.com

What began as a school project at Harvard has turned into an Internet phenomenon. Attracting more than 100 million unique visitors per month, Facebook is the most popular social networking site on the Net. With a Facebook account you can connect to millions of people all around the world. Chat, share photos, create a blog, post quick messages, or give a friend a poke (see Web site for details). More importantly, you can join various sub-networks within the Facebook community—networks that share your interests or career goals, that work in your industry or in an industry you'd like to transition to.

JibberJobber
www.jibberjobber.com

JibberJobber is a "Career Management" site, essentially a mash up of job search, career advice, and networking utilities. It is primarily designed to help you manage and organize your job search. With a free registration you can manage your network, take advantage of the job boards, and access the wealth of career and job search–related information in JibberJobber's library. Upgrading to a paid membership unlocks more storage space and other applications.

LinkedIn

www.linkedin.com

Discover the power of networking. When you join LinkedIn, you create a profile that summarizes your professional accomplishments. Through the LinkedIn network, you can find potential clients, service providers, subject experts, and partners who come recommended and discover inside connections that can help you land jobs. With more than 30 million subscribers, you are bound to know someone. Job openings include not only the name of the person posting the position but also anyone else you and your contacts may connect to in the organization. Additional services come with paid membership.

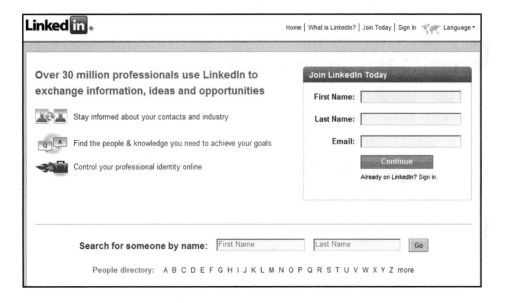

Plaxo

www.plaxo.com

Plaxo started as an online address book and then quickly jumped on the online networking wagon with the hopes of carving a niche. Using its Pulse technology, you create a kind of digital dashboard that keeps you up to date with what your friends, family, and contacts are doing and sharing. You can connect your own personal profile to other sites and applications you use on the Web, such as your blog, Flickr, and Twitter (although if these names seem unfamiliar to you, Plaxo may not be for you). You can also use its integrated address book and calendar features. As with the other sites in this section, Plaxo can help advance your career by helping you build and maintain your network. With more than 20 million users, odds are good you know someone out there that you haven't touched base with in a while, and that someone might just know of an opportunity for you.

Getting the Job

You've honed your Web job searching skills. Now, what's the best way to go about applying for, and landing, the perfect job? Check out the sites in the following sections for some tips that take you the rest of the way.

Resumes and Cover Letters

Read about electronic resumes in the Introduction to this book, and then extend your resume creation and cover letter skills by browsing the Web sites described here.

Louise Kursmark's Best Impression Blog

http://yourbestimpression.com/blog/

Louise Kursmark is the author of 18 books on resume writing, interviewing, and job search strategies and a founding board member of the Career Masters Institute. In this blog she shares with readers all of the tips and tactics she has learned in her experience as a resume expert. Everything in the blog is written by her, so you can be sure you are getting quality information and advice. Browse entries by topic or keyword, or just peruse the archives. Check out the sample resumes, especially if you are looking for an executive position. If you are in need of personal assistance, check out the services offered by Best Impressions Career Services, though be aware that such services aren't free.

eResumes & Resume Writing Services

www.eresumes.com

Resume help, tips, formats, examples, cover letters, online resumes, professional resumes, free resumes, e-resumes—you name it, this site has it.

For a new twist on resumes, check out this site's e-portfolios. Read about the process and concept, and then see some real examples.

How to Write a Resume

www.howtowritearesume.net/

There are several online resume-writing tools, many of them free. How to Write a Resume.net coaches you through the process in simple steps, taking much of the work out of formatting it. Use its "phrase builder" application to create action-oriented statements with keywords specific to your industry. Then use the sites integrated job search system to send your new resume out. Be sure to read the privacy policty before registering for any such service.

JobStar: Resumes & Cover Letters

http://jobstar.org/tools/resume/

JobStar's section on resumes and cover letters is categorized into several useful topics: What Is the Right Resume for Me?, Resume Samples, Selected Resume Resources on the Web, Resume Tips, Electronic Resume Banks, About Cover Letters, and Sample Cover Letters. If you don't know the difference between a chronological resume and a functional one, you've come to the right place.

Resume Power Blog

www.resumepower.com/blog/

> Resume Power is primarily a professional resume-writing service manned by a seasoned and knowledgeable staff. If you aren't interested in paying for a top-of-the-line resume makeover, you can still find good advice and free resources at the Resume Power Blog. Of particular interest here is the Resume Reading Room, which includes articles and tips on concerns specific to the resume writing process. Topics include resume formatting, entry-level resume tips, resumes for career changers, and writing resumes for specific career fields.

The Riley Guide: Resumes & Cover Letters

www.rileyguide.com/eresume.html

> A down-to-business site with some top-notch information. This particular page in the well-known Riley Guide (described later in this chapter) thoroughly explains what you should know before posting a resume online. It has plenty of pointers on content and formatting, choosing a job site, and staying cyber-safe. Links here take you to more job search information in the Riley Guide.

Vault.com: Sample Cover Letters

www.vault.com/nr/ht_list.jsp?ht_type=9

> On this page, Vault.com (described earlier) has a nice collection of cover letters for a range of positions, from amusement park employee to electrical engineer to investment banker to disaster relief worker. Visit other sites to learn about cover letter writing, and then see some cover letters in action.

Career Portfolios

A career portfolio is a collection of documents supporting your career aspirations, such as a resume, letters of recommendation, awards, certificates, articles, and so on. The Web sites in this section tell you what a career portfolio is, how it differs from a resume, how to create your own, and how to use it effectively.

Creating Your Portfolio

www2.biz.colostate.edu/career/portfolio.htm

> At this site, the Colorado State University College of Business spells out a simple process for assembling your own career portfolio. Learn what to include and what to leave out. Read some tips on portfolio formatting and appearance, as well as how to present your portfolio to prospective employers.

Portfolio Library

www.amby.com/kimeldorf/p_mk-toc.html

> Learn all about career portfolios at this Web site from author and educator Martin Kimeldorf. Although it's geared more toward teaching professionals, anyone can adapt the concepts described here to his or her own career areas. Topics in the Portfolio Library include Using Job Search Portfolios in an Uncertain Labor Market, Life-long Learning and Education Portfolios Meet Online, Professional Development Portfolio, Portfolio Creation Tips, and more. View a sample portfolio, along with a description of how and why it was assembled.

Visual CV

www.visualcv.com

> The curriculum vitae (or CV for short) is a fancy version of a resume, and the VisualCV is an even fancier one. Through the use of video, pictures, and an online portfolio, VisualCV turns your resume into a multimedia presentation, with informational pop-ups that provide background data on the companies you've worked at and the colleges you've attended. The Web site coaches you through the process of creating your own VisualCV and then helps you manage and distribute it, even helping you create and save multiple versions for different companies and career objectives. Best of all, creating an account is free. Web-based career portfolios are the wave of the future, and this site provides an easy way to take advantage of technology in your job search. Take the tour to see just how easy to use and powerful this portfolio-building tool can be.

Interviewing

After your resume has landed you that all-important job interview, you can get tips and advice on interview success from the following Web sites.

Interviewing Information
www.collegegrad.com/intv

> CollegeGrad.com is targeted at entry-level job seekers. This section of the site, packed with articles on interviewing successfully, is aimed especially at recent college graduates who might not have much interviewing experience. Get ideas on questions you can ask during interviews, check out the list of 50 standard entry-level interview questions and prepare your answers, learn how to have a successful phone interview, find out what to do after the interview, and more.

job-interview.net
www.job-interview.net

> This site provides a mix of free and for-fee information on job interviewing from the authors of *Best Answers to the 201 Most Frequently Asked Interview Questions*. Free information includes sample questions indexed by job functions, interviewing advice and tips, and a step-by-step interview success guide.

Monster Career Advice: Interview

http://career-advice.monster.com/interview-tips/home.aspx

> Take advice from the monster. This site is packed with informative articles on the art of being interviewed. It is organized into four sections, which can be accessed from the menu on the right: Prepare, Practice, Perform, and Follow Up. Each category has a list of informative, how-to articles for acing your interview on topics ranging from "Men's Interview Fashion Tips" to "How Do I Explain Getting Fired?" There's also a discussion board, which may come in handy to give you answers to specific questions.

Quintessential Careers: Guide to Job Interviewing Resources

www.quintcareers.com/intvres.html

> This collection of useful job interviewing resources includes tutorials, articles, and tools to prepare you for any type of interview. But activate your pop-up blocker first to reduce distractions. Start with the database of sample interview questions with "excellent sample responses" to find 109 of the most commonly asked questions and good ways to answer them. Take some practice interviews to see how your answers match up with the suggestions. Other great features include a job interview tutorial, a quiz to test your knowledge of the subject, and questions you can ask at an interview.

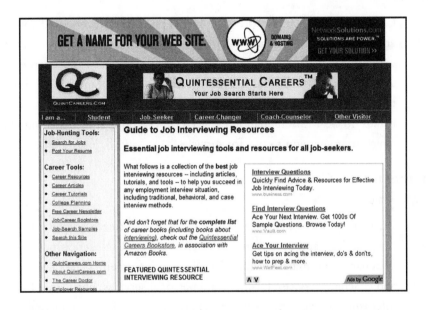

Career Clearinghouses

A clearinghouse is an index, directory, or listing of other Internet sites. Clearinghouses are good places to jump-start your research and save time, because someone has already conducted Internet searches, collected the best sites, written them up, and organized the results for you. Because clearinghouses are usually maintained by one (or just a few) individuals rather than by a large staff, their organization, focus, scope, and types of sites included differ. Links generally are organized into separate lists, allowing you to drill down easily to your desired topic—although some (usually smaller) clearinghouses might just arrange their links in alphabetical order. Some provide search capabilities, and others are meant simply for browsing.

Clearinghouse authors also like to give their stamp of approval to selected sites. These opinions often differ. You will notice, though, that the same links are often duplicated across different clearinghouses—which can give you an idea of the major sites in a particular area, or at least those that are most highly thought of by clearinghouse authors. You will likely want to investigate more than one of these sites to find relevant resources, because some list sites that do not appear on others.

Careers.org
www.careers.org

> Careers.org consists of more than 30,000 pages of career-related content and links to other Internet resources, organized by category. You can also search for jobs, find a career college, or read blog posts. Although it isn't as career-process-oriented as other clearinghouses, it can be a good place to search for resources for specific information. Be aware that the site makes no clear differentiation between general links and sponsored links, which try to get you to pay for services.

Internet Career Connection
http://iccweb.com

> Internet Career Connection is a clearinghouse of career-related information, services, and opportunities. Internet Career Connection provides searchable resource databanks for jobs in government, career counseling and coaching services, business and personal services, businesses for sale, internship and volunteer opportunities, and more. Each database listing

contains a site profile you can access for further information before jumping to the resource itself. Take a moment to read James Gonyea's *The Easy 10 Step Job Hunting Guide* for a simple "how to" approach to landing your next job.

Job-Hunt.org

www.job-hunt.org

Job-Hunt.org is owned by NETability Inc. and contains thousands of categorized, editor-selected links to career and job-hunting sites. Its posting policy contains some job-seeker-friendly criteria, including its decision not to list any sites that lack a privacy policy or that appear to be get-rich-quick or multilevel marketing scams. Each category contains annotated lists of links, the best of which are indicated by smiley-face icons. Be sure to read the introduction to each category for ideas on other sections to peruse and an explanation of the types of links you'll find included.

JobHuntersBible.com

www.jobhuntersbible.com

Dick Bolles created this Web site as a companion resource to his perennially popular book, *What Color Is Your Parachute?* Links here are divided into six major categories: The Internet, Research, Contacts, Counseling, Job Hunting, and Jobs and Resumes. Each section contains information from Bolles and further categories of Internet resources, themselves providing links with robust descriptions. You can click on Article Archive for a collection of career-related articles written by Bolles and other contributors. You also can learn about the latest edition of Bolles's book, including ordering information.

OneStop Job Search Guide: About.com

http://jobsearch.about.com/od/findajob/a/onestop.htm

About.com features experts whose job it is to pick the best resources and create added information in the form of articles and annotations. The OneStop Job Search Guide includes categorized links to career-related resources, from job databases to resume writing to relocation sites. Additional features include articles, forums, and a job search chat room. There's a lot here, and it can be hard to navigate, so feel free to use About.com's Search box if you need to locate something specific.

Quintessential Careers

www.quintcareers.com

> For an extensive list of links, visit Quintessential Careers. With more than 3,500 pages of college, career, and job search information, the content will keep you coming back. The site offers lots of approaches to finding the information you need. Try out the Career Toolkit for an organized, systematic approach to planning and managing your career using the best information QuintCareers has to offer. Post your resume, create a portfolio, search for jobs, subscribe to the e-zine, and even ask a career doctor for advice. (Note: The career doctor does not accept most forms of medical insurance.)

The Riley Guide: Employment Opportunities and Job Resources on the Internet

www.rileyguide.com

> One of the best and most comprehensive career and job information clearinghouses on the Internet, The Riley Guide has been online since 1994. Its simple, mostly ad-free design is a relaxing alternative to flashier sites. The site is deep in content; pick from the major categories listed on the front page, or use the A–Z index for an alphabetical list of the thousands of resources here. Each major category is broken into subcategories, and each of these suggests other related subcategories to try. The site was created and is maintained by Margaret F. Dikel, author of *The Guide to Internet Job Searching*.

CHAPTER 5

Researching Employer and Labor Market Information

One of the smartest things a job seeker can do is find out about an industry and an employer before walking into the interview—or, for that matter, applying for the job. Doing some research helps you make an informed decision and can leave your interviewers with an informed impression.

A number of resources help you find information on specific companies and the industries in which they operate. Read company press releases, find out the names of the key staff, scan professional journals, and get savvy about industry trends. You can find additional information through the job banks and career clearinghouses described in chapter 4.

Labor market information is data about workers, industries, employers, wages, and trends. It says a lot about the changing economy, so it is of interest to many. Job seekers can take note of declining or growing occupations, along with projected employment rates for the future, before making a career move. Entrepreneurs and new-business owners research wage information when planning their staffing structure.

For more detailed information on related resources, programs, and data for your state, see the list of state employment/workforce-development agencies in chapter 4. Also note the state-based career information systems mentioned in chapter 3, which base their projections on labor market data.

Finally, don't forget about informational interviewing. Identify and talk to people in the industries or fields in which you are interested. Do some homework first so that you have some background information and can ask intelligent questions. Also, don't be shy. People who love what they do love to tell others about it, especially as they may be approaching retirement. See the section "Informational Interviewing" in chapter 3 for some how-tos on getting started.

Researching Employers

Here are some general sites for researching employers online. Remember that one of the best sources of information on a company can be its own Web site. Search for employer Web sites by using the search engines and strategies discussed in the Introduction.

CorporateInformation.com

www.corporateinformation.com

Type a company's name into the search box on the front page to find information on it. You'll see a brief analysis as well as links to articles and company profiles (often for a fee) from other Web sites. Although much information is targeted at investors, you'll find useful background material for your job hunt as well. You can also pick a state to find information on every company the site covers in that state, or you can use an alphabetical list to browse corporations. This site is best for information on large companies.

Google News

http://news.google.com

Search and browse 4,500 English-language news sources from leading search engine Google. Find the most up-to-date news stories on specific companies, or simply go to the Business section to read current articles. This is a great way to stay current on industries and specific companies. You can find out what's going on before applying or in preparation for an interview. Articles stay in the index for 30 days.

Hoover's

www.hoovers.com/free/

Not to be confused with the makers of fine vacuums and sweepers, this
site provides overviews for more than 600 industries and 43,000 businesses. Search by keyword, industry, or geography, or use the alphabetical
listing to find a specific company. Basic information about each company
is free, including company overview and description, locations, financials,
press releases, and biggest competition. Additional information is available
for a fee or with a paid subscription. But the free information should be
enough for most job seekers looking to see whether a company is a good
fit or prepping for an interview.

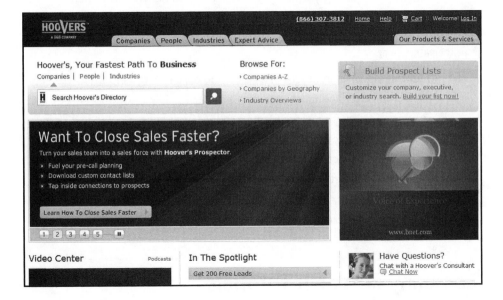

One Day, One Job

www.onedayonejob.com/

Ever wondered what it was like to work at Boston's Children Museum?
Or to write for the Onion? Or to be a part of the Sea Turtle Restoration
Project? If the answer is no (as odds would have it), you should still take
the time to visit One Day, One Job. This blog provides an insider look
at unique and exciting entry-level jobs and internships for recent college
graduates. Each day the site editors profile a new employer with entry-
level positions available, many of them companies that you might not have

heard of. You can also use the site's career tools for links to recommended books, articles, and Web sites. While not the most comprehensive way to research employers, it's worth subscribing just to see what new opportunities arise.

SuperPages

www.superpages.com

SuperPages is an electronic yellow pages—with a twist. Search for U.S. businesses by keyword, name, or location, or browse by category. Each listing contains contact information as well as a Web site link when available, plus a map and driving directions. Register to create your own directory of saved listings, which you can access online from anywhere.

ThomasNet

www.thomasnet.com/

ThomasNet is an industrial search engine designed to help industrial suppliers and buyers connect on a national, regional, and local level. You can conduct a geographic search for a product or service, a company, or a brand name, or you can browse through category listings. Check out the searchable Product News, with the latest information on industries with archives organized by category. Although the site is meant largely for locating suppliers, it's a useful way for job seekers to locate and become informed about companies in their industry as well.

Company Research Tutorials

For tips and instructions on researching employers, check out these Web sites.

Industry Research Desk

www.virtualpet.com/industry/

Another site that emphasizes free sources, the Industry Research Desk features an 18-step process that walks you through researching a specific company or industry. This is helpful background information to have before going on that interview or applying for that position. A ton of links to useful resources are included among the steps, so take some time to explore. You'll also find ideas on print resources that can be useful; you can find many of these at your local public or college library.

Researching Companies Online

www.learnwebskills.com/company/

> Here's an online tutorial for finding no-fee company and industry information on the Web. Topics include locating company home pages, monitoring company news, learning about an industry, identifying international business resources, researching nonprofit organizations, and much more. A sure bet for sharpening your research skills.

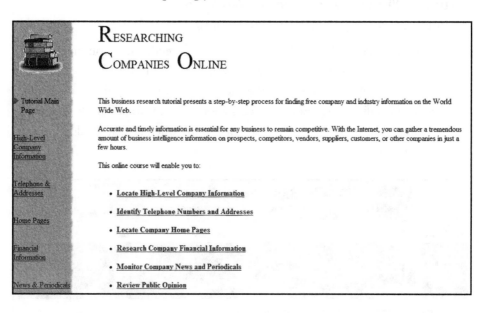

Riley Guide: Business & Employer Research

www.rileyguide.com/employer.html

> This section of the respected Riley Guide provides another useful resource for your job search, this one focusing on researching employers on the Internet. Categories include How to Research Employers, What It's Like to Work At, Business Directories/Corporate Profiles, Business Research Collections, and Know the Industry Codes. This section can also point you toward stock market and financial information, as well as business and employer rankings.

Company Rankings

Lists are fun, and this section has a few that might aid you in your career research. A number of magazines and Web sites publish rankings of the "best" companies according to different criteria, many of which are updated yearly. Like the *U.S. News & World Report* college rankings mentioned in chapter 1, you'll want to take these light-heartedly, but they can give you an idea of what makes some organizations more highly regarded than others, and what to look for in a potential employer and why.

Fortune: 100 Best Companies to Work For

http://money.cnn.com/magazines/fortune/bestcompanies/

> *Fortune* initiated the whole company-ranking trend, and it continues to create its annual list of the 100 best companies to work for every year going back to 1998. Unfortunately, the site wants you to subscribe to the magazine (at a discounted rate) to access a lot of the information. But there's enough free info here to help you determine whether that would be a value for you.

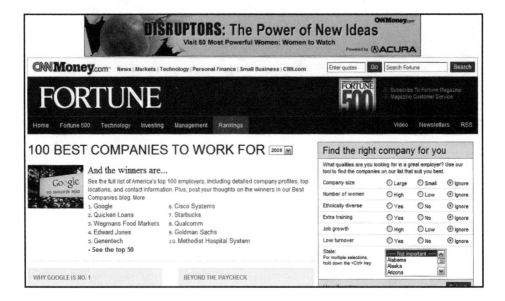

Price's List of Lists

www.specialissues.com/lol/

>Price's List of Lists is a database of rankings of companies, people, and resources. It was started by Gary Price in 1998 and now is sponsored by SpecialIssues.com. No membership is required to browse through the lists. They show the periodical source, article name, whether the article has a fee, and the year of publication. For example, you can find the top 100 school districts and college facilities ranked by size, the top 50 propane industry retailers, and the top 100 fitness facility companies, to name just a few. The collection of periodicals that the lists are based on gives you an idea of the breadth of information covered here. And if you ever want to know who the top-earning dead celebrity is, you can find that out here as well.

Working Mother: 100 Best Companies

www.workingmother.com/?service=vpage/109

>*Working Mother* has been compiling its annual list of the 100 best companies for working mothers for more than 20 years. The list provides company profiles and handy links to each company's Web site so that you can find further information. The top ten list includes brief information on why each was selected. The Hall of Fame list includes companies that have been named to the 100 Best for 15 years or more and that appear in the current 100 Best list.

Researching Labor Market Information

Labor market information online has become more accessible and user-friendly over the years. Even better, almost all of it is made freely available by the government and other sources.

Government Sources

Most key national labor market indicators are developed by federal and state agencies. Use the government sources in this section to research industry employment estimates and projections, occupational data, labor force statistics, unemployment rates, employment hours and earnings, the consumer price index, demographic and socioeconomic data, population estimates and projections, business cycle indicators, and more. In addition, the Web sites described in this section provide information on federal programs and initiatives that affect the U.S. workforce, such as the Workforce Investment Act of 1998. If this sounds like a lot to digest, don't worry. Almost every site has search or sorting tools to help you find the information of most interest to you. To view many of the files on these sites, you need Adobe Acrobat Reader. It's available for free from the Adobe Web site at www. adobe.com/products/acrobat/readstep2.html.

FedStats

www.fedstats.gov

> If you don't know which agency keeps the statistics you need, this is a great place to begin. FedStats is the government's portal to statistics from more than 100 federal agencies. You can access the data here in a number of ways, from an A–Z index to information organized by state to a search across all these agencies' Web sites at once. You'll find an alphabetical list of agencies, with a brief description of the mission and the key types of statistics compiled by each. Check out the list of kids' pages for a fun place to start.

U.S. Bureau of Economic Analysis (BEA)

www.bea.gov

> The Bureau of Economic Analysis of the U.S. Department of Commerce is a major producer and compiler of economic, business-cycle, and labor-market data. BEA provides data and articles on regional, national, and international economic issues. Regional information includes state and local-area personal income data. National information covers personal income, the gross domestic product, corporate profits, and more. International information includes balance of payments, U.S. direct investment abroad, and foreign direct investment in the U.S. You'll also find articles that summarize and explain all this data, as well as an A–Z index,

FAQs, and even a glossary. Odds are, you won't need most of this information, but it can help to see how the industry you are working in (or want to work in) is doing, or what the labor market is like in your area.

U.S. Census Bureau

www.census.gov

Did you know that as of this writing, there are 305,653,169 people in the United States…give or take a few? The U.S. Census Bureau, another agency of the U.S. Department of Commerce, is a premiere site for socioeconomic and demographic data. Web site information is grouped into topics titled People, Business, Geography, Newsroom, and Special Topics. You can search the Web site or the FAQs by keyword. If you don't know what you're looking for, or if you want to see it all, you can browse through an alphabetical subject index. Cool stuff here includes U.S. and world population clocks, state and county profiles, economic surveys and indicators, and TIGER, the coast-to-coast digital map base. You'll definitely want to check out the American FactFinder, an interactive database tool that allows you to easily access area-specific general, social, economic, and housing statistics from Census 2000.

U.S. Census Bureau: Statistical Abstract of the United States

www.census.gov/compendia/statab/

The Statistical Abstract of the United States is a good example of the quantity, quality, and accessibility of information available from the U.S. Census Bureau. The section on labor force, employment, and earnings covers everything from unemployment statistics to the number of employed workers actively seeking new jobs. This information is broken down by age, sex, level of education, and occupational category. The Statistical Abstract is the resource of choice for the most useful U.S. social and economic data.

U.S. Department of Labor

www.dol.gov

The U.S. Department of Labor's Web site highlights current news. It also features quick access to popular services such as the *Occupational Outlook Handbook,* the Family and Medical Leave Act, and Career Voyage (click on Job Seekers under Audiences to find the most pertinent information). The site is nicely organized with links for specific audiences. One click takes you to the more than 20 links for job and training information, as well as resources for layoffs, wage and hour laws, workplace safety, retirement and health benefits, and disability information. You can use the standard search or A–Z index tools to quickly locate specific information.

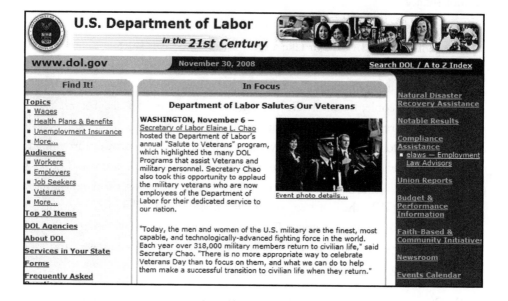

U.S. Department of Labor Bureau of Labor Statistics (BLS)

www.bls.gov

The U.S. Bureau of Labor Statistics is a prime source of nationwide labor market information. It also has a significant amount of information at the state and local level. BLS has extensive Internet offerings, including inflation and consumer spending, employment and unemployment statistics, a variety of productivity indexes, employee benefits and compensation surveys, and even career information for kids. You can also access regional BLS offices for information targeted to your area to get statistics on the regional economy by state and metropolitan area (such as the current unemployment rate in your city or employment statistics by industry). This site is searchable and contains an A–Z index to help you find needed information. Or you can drill down through the categories listed on the front page (including demographics, occupations, wages, earnings, benefits, and more) to locate your specific topic of interest.

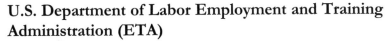

U.S. Department of Labor Employment and Training Administration (ETA)

www.doleta.gov

> The U.S. Department of Labor Employment and Training Administration is the primary agency for federal workforce development programs. Much of the Web site content is aimed at federal and state professionals working in employment and training programs. But if you're a job seeker, check out the Find Job and Career Information section for resources to help you start a new job, make long-term career plans, research job opportunities, deal with job loss, and find training to acquire new skills. Employers can get information on government incentives and assistance and employment resources. You'll also find links to state and local resources such as one-stop centers, training providers, and more.

Workforce Development

Workforce development concerns initiatives and programs addressing the growth and maintenance of an educated, skilled workforce. These programs typically are coordinated among multiple public, private, and nonprofit employment and training providers and are funded through the federal government.

Workforce ATM

www.naswa.org

> Workforce ATM is a service of the National Association of State Work Force Agencies, the national organization of state administrators of unemployment insurance, employment and training services, and labor market information programs. This Web site helps track information on related initiatives, providing links to each state's workforce development and employer services agencies. It also features news and headlines on topics from dislocated workers to veterans' services. Although much of the information here is for members only, the public sections of the site provide a great way to keep up with workforce development news and information.

CHAPTER 6

Military Careers

The U.S. military is one of the country's largest employers, including service members on full-time active duty, part-time reservists, and National Guard members. Each year, the military hires more than 365,000 new enlisted and officer personnel. The ongoing War on Terror and increasing threats at home and abroad ensure that the military will continue to be on the lookout for new recruits and will offer incentives for joining the ranks.

Learn about the wide variety of military career options by exploring the sites in this chapter, which describe military recruiting, the different branches, service academies, reserves and the National Guard, civilian job opportunities, and even resources for military spouses. You'll also find sites that will be helpful as you make the jump back to civilian employment after your military career.

In addition to helping you learn whether the military is for you, the information at these sites can get you up to speed before you sit down to talk to a recruiter. Doing your research always pays off.

Beyond the learning opportunities that serving in the military offers, the military also sponsors a number of lifelong and distance learning options for current and retired service members. You can find information on these programs in chapter 2.

General Information

About the U.S. Military

http://usmilitary.about.com

About.com scores again with a wide collection of military resources from current news to recruitment, pay and benefits, off-duty information, and life after the military. Sign up for a free weekly e-newsletter, see the glossary of military terms, get answers to FAQs, and peruse the list of how-tos (such as how to survive boot camp or how to ship your vehicle overseas).

ASVAB Career Exploration Program

http://asvabprogram.com

The ASVAB's (Armed Services Vocational Aptitude Battery) main purpose is to show students and potential recruits where their aptitudes and abilities lie, helping them make the best military, educational, and career choices. This comprehensive site supports the ASVAB Career Exploration Program, which is used in many schools to help students make these choices. All new recruits must take the exam to determine which military careers they are eligible for. Bear in mind that most of the site's features are accessible only after you have taken the ASVAB.

Careers in the Military

www.careersinthemilitary.com/

> Uncertain about a career in the military? This site, developed by the Department of Defense, is an ideal starting point for military career research. Browse careers by job family, get insider perspectives from active military personnel (just what does a ship officer do?), even search for military jobs "outside the norm," such as meteorological specialist and graphic designer. Each job leads to a short description, a bulleted list of work tasks, a list of helpful attributes, descriptions of the training provided and the work environment, and even a description of the types of civilian jobs this military career would prepare you for.

Milblogging

www.milblogging.com/

> As part of Military.com (see following entry), Milblogging started as the pet project of National Guardsman Jean-Paul Borda. While deployed in Afghanistan, Borda used a blog to stay in contact with his family and friends. Wanting to create an easy way to find and take part in military blogs around the world, he created this aggregator site. Milblogging is essentially a database of more than 2,000 military blogs in 41 different countries. It includes blogs written by spouses, veterans, current personnel, reporters, military parents, and other groups. Many of the blogs are written by troops on the front lines. Blogs give you an inside look at what life is like for people in the military and those around them. It can help you keep up on hot topics and ongoing debates. Most importantly, reading the posts from Milblogs can help you to make an informed decision about whether the military is a good career option for you. Peruse the top 100 Milblogs; find blogs by branch of the military; or search by country, language, or gender. Registration is free.

Military.com

www.military.com

> Military.com claims to be the largest online military destination. Unique offerings here include a buddy finder and community center, a military scholarship database, a veterans' job board, a military mentor network, military news, a military reunion planning guide and posting service, and

even a store where you can purchase military supplies (need a new pair of night-vision goggles?). How to join the military is spelled out for you in a ten-step process, with recruiter links, an ASVAB practice test, and discussion boards offering firsthand advice and knowledge. And if you get tired of reading, you can visit the photo and video gallery or download one of the military's new video games.

My Future
www.myfuture.com

Here you can sign up to receive more information on branches of the service that interest you, take work interest and personality quizzes, and find out about military education funding. This Web site has information on general career exploration, job search techniques, and money management, but its strength lies in the military career information. Learn about skills training and educational opportunities, and get answers to common military questions. It's a good stop on the research trail for someone considering a military career.

Stars and Stripes
www.stripes.com

To get a sense of being in the military, read what U.S. military personnel are reading. *Stars and Stripes* is a Department of Defense–authorized daily newspaper distributed overseas for the U.S. military community. Editorially independent of interference from outside its editorial chain of command, it provides commercially available U.S. and world news and objective staff-produced stories relevant to the military community in a balanced, fair, and accurate manner. Your knowledge of current military events is sure to impress a recruiter.

Today's Military
www.todaysmilitary.com

Today's Military is a good first stop if you (or your son or daughter) are considering a career in the military. Formerly the Military Career Guide Online, this site provides general information on military life and the rewards of a military career. In addition, you can browse through officer and enlisted jobs organized by career category. Each description includes information on areas such as duties, helpful attributes, training provided, and work environment.

U.S. Military Branches of Service

Following are specific sites for the Air Force, Army, Coast Guard, Marines, and Navy.

Air Force

Air Force Link/Careers

www.af.mil/careers/

Information on careers for enlisted personnel, officers, civilians, and retirees can be found in the Careers section of Air Force Link, the official Web site for the Air Force. Look through current employment opportunities and find out about pay scales, promotions, retirement pay, and all the other details of an Air Force career. For plenty more Air Force information, visit other sections of Air Force Link, including News, TV, Radio, Photos, Letters, History, and more.

U.S. Air Force

www.airforce.com

This official recruiting Web site for the U.S. Air Force requires the latest Macromedia Flash and other multimedia plugins to capture the excitement of an Air Force career. Take the video guide for starters, or browse through career fields by category to find the one that's right for you, and find out about all the benefits of an Air Force career. You can also sign up to receive more information, chat online with an advisor, or view videos of Air Force operations and personnel. Also available in Spanish.

Army

GoArmy.com

www.goarmy.com

The official U.S. Army recruiting site provides an overview of Army life through articles, photos, and video interviews. Watch a little Army Strong TV to get a glimpse of basic training or see what life is like on a military post. Browse job categories or search for a specific career. Learn about enlistment incentives, officer training, college education benefits, and specialized opportunities such as the Army Band, Chaplain Corps, Judge Advocate General's Corps, and Special Forces. Chat with a recruiter online, or send for additional information.

U.S. Army

www.army.mil

While less flashy than its recruiting site (above), the official U.S. Army site includes tons of information for anyone interested in an Army career. You could spend hours browsing through the news and links here, or search for the specific information you need (use the A–Z guide if you aren't sure what you're looking for). Pick the Career Management link to find out about Army careers, including enlisted, officer, and civilian opportunities.

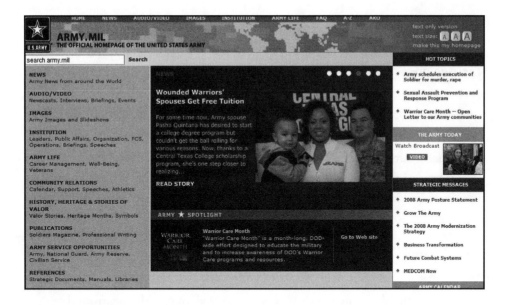

Coast Guard

U.S. Coast Guard

www.uscg.mil/

> Part of the U.S. Department of Homeland Security, the Coast Guard provides links on its official site to news, jobs, services, history, Coast Guard missions, and more. Its motto is "Semper Paratus" (Always Ready). This site provides all the details you need about this service branch.

U.S. Coast Guard Recruiting

www.gocoastguard.com

> Click on "Find Your Fit" to choose from enlisted, officer, and reserve opportunities with the Coast Guard, and find information on civilian careers and scholarship opportunities, at this official recruiting site. You can also sign up to receive more information or locate a recruiter near you.

Marines

Marines.com
www.marines.com

> Marines.com is the official recruiting site for the U.S. Marine Corps, and it features a virtual tour of life in the Marine Corps. While the tour is exhaustive, including everything from the history of the Marines to the state-of-the-art gear they use, there's a search engine and a site map if you are looking for more specific information. Find out here about training, job opportunities, educational options, and more.

U.S. Marine Corps
www.marines.mil

> The official Marine Corps Web site covers all things Marine, from the band to news to history, video, and images of the Corps. Search for a desired topic, or simply browse the main page for links to current stories and information. There's plenty to keep you coming back.

Navy

U.S. Navy
www.navy.mil

> Welcome aboard the official U.S. Navy Web site, your one-stop shop for information on everything from careers to ships. Get briefed on the latest Navy news on the home page. For specific information, the information index and site search are your doorways to finding all the facts you need.

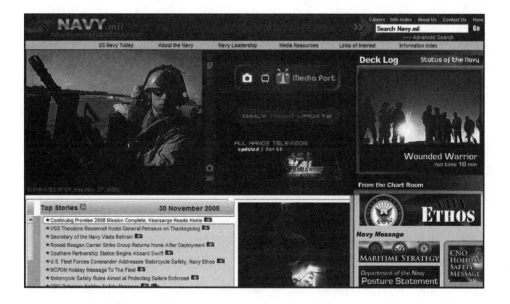

U.S. Navy Opportunities

www.navy.com

"Accelerate your life" at the Navy's official recruitment site. If a military career is in your future, speed up your search by exploring all the information here, including the Life Accelerator, an online self-assessment that will match your interests to careers in the Navy. Also look over descriptions of Navy careers, benefits, and educational opportunities. Get answers to your specific questions through the message board, which has a special thread for parents.

U.S. Service Academies

The service academies give you a four-year college education while preparing you for a career as an officer in the armed forces. Strict admissions guidelines consider such factors as U.S. citizenship (with certain exceptions), academic performance, standardized test scores, extracurricular activities, athletic ability, age, marital status, and moral character. All but the Coast Guard Academy require that you be nominated by a member of Congress or another qualified nominator.

Air Force Academy Admissions Center

http://academyadmissions.com

Geared specifically toward students (and their parents), this well-organized
site walks you through all aspects of applying for admission to the U.S.
Air Force Academy, from finding out about academic majors to applying
online. Parents will appreciate the parents' guide, full of information
to help them understand what the Academy has to offer their son or
daughter.

U.S. Air Force Academy

www.usafa.af.mil

This official site of the U.S. Air Force Academy in Colorado Springs,
Colorado, offers information on all aspects of student life, academics, and
programs. Highlights include a home page packed with the latest academy
news, information for visitors, descriptions and a photo gallery of cadet
life, and much more.

U.S. Coast Guard Academy

www.cga.edu

Learn all about the Coast Guard Academy in New London, Connecticut,
at its official Web site. Here you can find information on the Academy,
from an overview to an online application form to FAQs. News, history,
candidate profiles, and information on cadet life and academics can help
you decide whether there's a Coast Guard career in your future.

U.S. Merchant Marine Academy

www.usmma.edu

Find out what it takes to be admitted to the U.S. Merchant Marine
Academy at Kings Point, New York. Read online about admissions, academic requirements, midshipman life, athletics, and more. Or browse the
downloadable PDF catalog to read at your leisure.

U.S. Military Academy (West Point)

www.usma.edu

Current news events are featured on the home page of the U.S. Military
Academy. To learn about its 200-year tradition, start with About the

Academy to explore its programs, including academic, physical, military, and moral-ethical components. A site search and FAQs help you drill down to the information you need.

U.S. Naval Academy

www.usna.edu

This is the official site for the U.S. Naval Academy in Annapolis, Maryland. Browse through the announcements and links listed here, or use the search or site index to find specific information. Admissions information includes a handy step-by-step description of the process to help you become a well-prepared applicant.

National Guard

The National Guard serves the dual mission of supporting the armed forces in times of war and maintaining order at a state level during emergencies. Find out about the different branches and about full- and part-time soldier and civilian opportunities at the sites described here. Read through the primary Guard sites described in this section for good, general information, and then visit the recruiting sites for specifics on signing up.

Air National Guard

Air National Guard (ANG)

www.ang.af.mil

> If your future is up in the air, the Air National Guard may provide some options. This official site of the Air National Guard includes recruiting information, the history of the ANG, full-time and part-time career opportunities, and links to ANG units across the country.

Air National Guard Recruitment

www.goang.com

> Explore recruiting information and career opportunities with the Air National Guard, get questions answered through an online chat, request information from your local recruiter, and find out the benefits that even a part-time Air National Guard career can bring. You can also search for open positions by state or keyword, get the real scoop on basic training, or take a break in the online arcade.

Army National Guard

Army National Guard

www.arng.ngb.army.mil

> The Army National Guard is one component of the Army, which consists of the active Army (described earlier), the Army National Guard, and the Army Reserve (described in the next section). This official site describes the Guard's unique dual mission of both federal and state roles, as well as extensive information on the Guard's organization, current activities, leadership, and history. Check the FAQs for answers to specific questions or use the search engine to zero in on the information you want.

Army National Guard Recruitment

www.1800goguard.com

> The official Army National Guard online recruiting center includes information for students and graduates, veterans, medical professionals,

parents, and educators. Find out about the history of the Guard, learn about basic and career training, and get the lowdown on money for college as well as salary and benefit information. Use a quick link to contact a recruiter or sign up for e-mail Guard updates.

The Reserves

The Armed Forces Reserves are military personnel who are not normally on full-time active duty but who are trained and equipped to be mobilized during a war or national crisis. High school graduates can apply to ROTC (Reserve Officer Training Corps) programs to earn a college education while also receiving officer training in their military branch.

Air Force

U.S. Air Force Reserve
www.afreserve.com

> Explore the missions of the U.S. Air Force Reserve at its official Web site. Site tools include a recruiter locator, live chat, FAQs, and game and screen-saver downloads. A wide range of information is available here, from the benefits of joining the Air Force Reserve to reports on air show events and Air Force Reserve Touring Car racing.

U.S. Air Force Reserve Officer Training Corps (ROTC)
www.afrotc.com

> More than 1,000 U.S. colleges and universities participate in the Air Force ROTC program. Through the program, you can get the money you need for college and earn a degree while working toward becoming an officer in the U.S. Air Force. Get information on the program, read about admissions standards and requirements, or apply online for a scholarship. Videos of individual cadets give you an idea of what the program is like, and you can explore Air Force careers to see what opportunities await you after graduation. Parents will also appreciate the special section geared toward them.

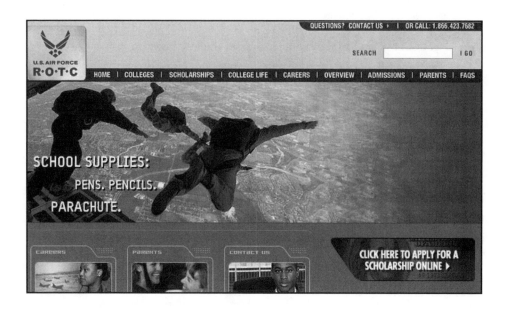

Army

U.S. Army Reserve

www.goarmy.com/reserve/nps/

> Get an in-depth look at the types of training you can receive as an Army Reserve soldier; learn about education benefits, cash bonuses, and lifestyle benefits; read a featured profile of a reservist; and find out what Reserve jobs are available to you. You can chat online with a recruiter or contact one locally, e-mail a question, or request an information packet be sent to you.

U.S. Army Reserve Officer Training Corps (ROTC)

www.goarmy.com/rotc/

> Army ROTC is an elective curriculum you take along with your required college classes. Army ROTC offers two-, three-, and four-year college scholarships to qualified high school seniors or current college students, plus you graduate into an Army career with a rank of Second Lieutenant. Get all the specifics here and learn from the experiences of officers who launched their Army careers through the program. Find participating schools, research scholarships, consider career paths, or check out the profiles of students currently participating in the program.

Coast Guard

U.S. Coast Guard Reserve

www.uscg.mil/reserve/

> Get the whole story on the U.S. Coast Guard Reserve as well as recruiting information. Here you can read *The Reservist* magazine, keep up on current events, and learn about training opportunities, including the Reserve Enlisted Basic Indoctrination (REBI) course in Cape May, New Jersey.

Navy

U.S. Navy Reserve

www.navyreserve.com

> The top five reasons people join the Navy Reserve are patriotism, career advancement, camaraderie, leadership skills, and physical fitness. If you identify with these, find out more here about entry requirements, entrance programs, enlisted and officer opportunities, pay, and benefits. The home page lists in-demand careers that the Navy Reserve will train you for. Profiles of current reservists provide great information on actual experiences in the Reserve.

U.S. Navy Reserve Officer Training Corps (NROTC)

https://www.nrotc.navy.mil

> If you aspire to be a naval aviator, flight officer, special warfare officer, submarine officer, or surface warfare officer, the NROTC may be your career ticket. Successful applicants are awarded scholarships through a highly competitive national selection process. They receive full tuition, books, fees, and other financial benefits at many of the country's leading colleges and universities. Upon graduation, students become commissioned officers. This site describes the full range of career options.
> After you have applied, you can revisit this site to check your application's status.

Civilian Opportunities in (or for) the Military

Soldiers are not the only contributors to the effectiveness of our armed forces. Check out the numbers of civilians employed to appreciate this job market. The military relies on civilian employees to fulfill roles not covered through military positions. Find out here about civilian positions you may not have known existed.

Air Force Personnel Center (AFPC) Civilian Employment
https://ww2.afpc.randolph.af.mil/resweb/

> This page is designed to be a one-stop shopping list for civilian employees and job seekers. A great time saver, it clearly describes what services are available to job seekers through the Air Force Personnel Center. The Air Force employs more than 150,000 civilians in a full range of occupations, including financial management, information management, public affairs, engineering, computers/communications, sports/fitness recreation management, contracting, logistics, and education, to name a few. Expand your career options and thinking by poking around here.

Army and Air Force Exchange Service (AAFES) Employment Opportunities
http://odin.aafes.com/Employment/default.asp

> AAFES employs more than 45,000 civilians in base or post exchanges on U.S. military installations worldwide. AAFES recruits for entry-level and management positions in retail, information systems, finance and accounting, logistics, food service/restaurant management, contracting and procurement, and occasionally other career fields. If you're married to an active-duty military member, you may qualify for a spouse employment hiring preference.

Army Civilian Personnel On-Line
http://cpol.army.mil

> Civilians have been working for the U.S. military since the Revolutionary War. With more than 250,000 employees, you can bet there's a job opportunity for you here somewhere. In today's Army, civilians work in a wide

range of occupations, including scientist, engineer, administrator, physician, information technologist, childcare director, program analyst, recreation specialist, customer service representative, and many more. The site lets you search for vacancy announcements by keyword, location, general occupation, and pay grade. You can also submit an electronic resume with the site's Resume Builder program, with online help provided.

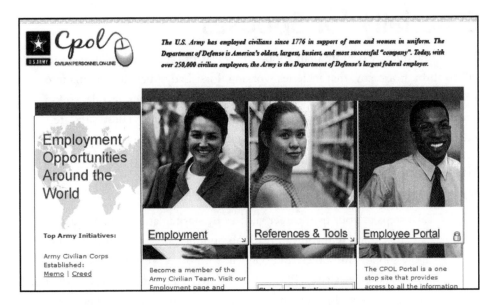

Civilian On-line Applicant Staffing Tool (COAST)

www.uscg.mil/civilianhr/

More than 6,000 civilian jobs exist in the U.S. Coast Guard, including professional, administrative, technical, trades and labor, full-time, part-time, and student positions. Although the site now uses USAJobs to search and apply for current job openings, you can still find out about the kinds of career opportunities available to you here.

Department of the Navy's Civilian Hiring and Recruitment Tool

https://chart.donhr.navy.mil

What could a librarian in Sicily, a pharmacist in Oak Harbor, Washington, and a social worker in Spain have in common? They may all be civilian employees of the U.S. Navy or Marine Corps. According to the Department of Navy Civilian Human Resources, more than 180,000 civilians are employed in Naval and Marine Corps activities throughout the world. Get the scoop on the jobs at this site with its searchable job opportunity database. Then create a personal account to use the resume builder and create automated job search agents.

Especially for Spouses

Being in the military is more than a job—it's a way of life, as any military spouse will confirm. For many, that includes working. First Lady Michelle Obama intends to make serving the needs of military spouses prominent on her agenda, so look for more initiatives on the executive level in the coming years. These sites are geared to the unique and specific needs of military families.

Military Spouse Career Center

www.military.com/spouse

Take steps to your own career success by starting at Military Spouse Career Center. Here you can read job hunting tips, search for jobs, find family support resources, and connect with others through discussion boards and a newsletter. Plus, if you create an account, you can post your resume online and get updates on the latest listings. The Military Spouse Career Center Web site is operated by Monster and Military.com under contract with the Department of Defense, so the amount of information and number of resources here should come as no surprise.

MilSpouse.org

www.milspouse.org

If you are married to the military, this is the site for you. MilSpouse.org is a clearinghouse of employment, education, and relocation information and resources addressing the special needs of military families. It's sponsored by the Department of Defense and the Department of Labor. Locate your military base welcome center, get tips on preparing for a job campaign, learn about educational opportunities, find out where you can turn for relocation assistance—it's all here.

MyArmyLifeToo.com

www.myarmylifetoo.com

> This site aims to be the "Web site of choice for Army families," and you'll find plenty to back that up. The topics range from work and careers to lifelong learning, money matters, home and family life, and managing deployment. You can also find specific resources based on whether your spouse is a member of the active Army, the Army National Guard, or the Army Reserve.

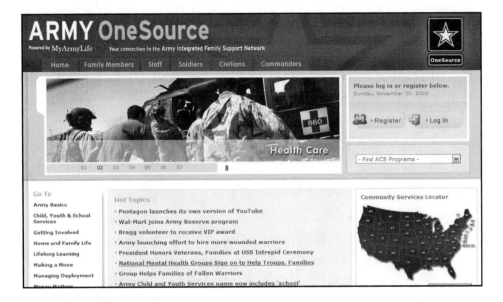

Post-Military Careers

Military and government-funded employment assistance programs help active military personnel make the jump back into civilian employment. In addition, other organizations have stepped in to help connect veterans with employers. All of them are putting the power of the Internet to work to make information and services readily available and accessible.

Corporate Gray Online

www.corporategray.com/

> Corporate Gray Online exists for one purpose: to provide free military transition services for veterans. Employers that use Corporate Gray Online

understand the military environment and search the database of online resumes for job candidates with the mix of skills and experience that fits their needs. Post your resume to apply online with hundreds of "military-friendly" companies, or make an in-person visit to one of the military job fairs that Corporate Gray sponsors across the U.S. You can also sign up to have new job listings matching your criteria sent to your e-mail inbox. If that's not enough, you can find training and educational opportunities for veterans, as well as helpful tips on relocation, links to sites for doing company research, FAQs, and other job search resources.

Department of Defense (DoD) TransPortal

www.dodtransportal.dod.mil/

This portal for transitioning military provides information on DoD transition assistance services, including contact information for the different branches, a preseparation guide, and mini-courses on conducting a job search and applying for jobs online. You can also find links to Internet job search sites and corporate recruiting sites.

elaws Advisors: Veterans' Issues

www.dol.gov/elaws/veterans.html

The elaws Advisors from the U.S. Department of Labor are interactive e-tools that provide easy-to-understand information about a number of federal employment laws as well as other helpful information. Veterans' Issues explains federal laws on reemployment rights, veterans' preference, and federal contract compliance. In addition, the e-VETS Resource Advisor provides a list of Web sites most relevant to your specific needs and interests, such as job search tools and tips, employment openings, career assessment, education and training, and benefits and special services available to veterans. The REALifelines Advisor is designed to help wounded and injured veterans find online resources and contact information for one-on-one employment assistance.

Transition Assistance Online

www.taonline.com

About 200,000 service members each year transition from active duty. If you're among them, or if you're among the thousands of veterans, reservists, retirees, guardsmen, and working spouses who are looking for new civilian jobs and other career opportunities, this site is for you. After setting up a free account, you can not only search for job openings using multiple search criteria, but you also can use the online resume and resume management tools. Furthermore, you can sign up for an electronic newsletter that provides information on job-seeker services for the military community, or check out the other Transition Tools for additional career advice.

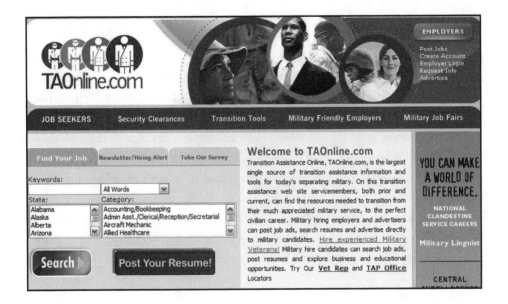

Veteran Career Network

http://benefits.military.com/vcn/search.do

The goal of the Veteran Career Network is to help veterans capitalize on the training they received in the military by connecting them with employers that value this type of training. You can view the career profiles of other veterans in the network; contact network members in specific companies, locations, or careers; or post your own profile for others to view. You can also conduct a job search, post a resume, and use the skills translator to translate your MOS, Rate, AFSC, or designator into civilian terms. The Veteran Career Network, from Military.com, opened its doors, appropriately enough, on Veterans' Day in 2005.

Veterans' Employment and Training Service (VETS)

www.dol.gov/vets/

All veterans should be aware of the Veterans' Employment and Training Service (VETS) in the U.S. Department of Labor, the federal agency working on their behalf. That said, information of most interest to the individual is better found at elaws Advisors: Veterans' Issues (described earlier in this section). What you will find here are descriptions on the programs, laws, and regulations administered by the agency.

VetJobs.com

www.vetjobs.com

"Veterans Make the Best Employees." So says VetJobs, whose mission it is to make sure those future employees find the jobs they need. VetJobs.com helps vets understand how to approach the civilian job market and helps employers appreciate veterans' skills and capabilities. Search the jobs database, or post your resume online to let potential employers find you. You can also subscribe to a free monthly e-mail newsletter to get tips on using the site and making the transition. Also check out resources and organizations for additional support, or see the employment assistance category for tips on interviewing and job hunting in the civilian sector. The site has the exclusive endorsement of the U.S. Veterans of Foreign Wars (VFW).

CHAPTER 7

Self-Employment and Small Business

Thinking about self-employment? You're far from alone. According to the U.S. Census Bureau, over 10.5 million Americans are self-employed, 40 percent of them in management, professional, and related occupations.

Many self-employed people start the process by working as a free agent or contractor and then extend the concept to create their own business. (For more on free agency, see chapter 8.) Whether you work from home as a "SOHO-ist" (we'll explain later) or create a business that grows to employ tens or hundreds of people, owning your own business puts you in control of your employment. Independence is the most common reason cited for going the self-employment route.

Being self-employed, however, doesn't mean you have to go it alone. These days you can join a networking group or professional association, receive free e-newsletters, read business magazines online, locate an e-mail or face-to-face mentor, find specific information for little or no cost, post questions or comments in discussion groups, chat online with others like yourself, or participate in a live tele-discussion.

The Web sites in this chapter provide you with convenient, quality information not only to help you make good business decisions but also to connect you with others and stay informed, motivated, and inspired.

Government Resources for Small Businesses

What did we do before the Internet, especially when it comes to finding government information? Federal, state, and local government has gotten much better at using the Internet to make the information we need easier to find. This is especially good news for business owners sorting their way through regulations and requirements.

Business.gov
www.business.gov

Visit Business.gov for one-stop access to federal information and services. Mine for information either by business topic (Business Law, Finance, Licenses and Permits, Taxes, etc.), or by keyword search. Check out the 10 Steps to Starting a Business for a quick list of resources about the phases in the process. Because more than 22 federal organizations assist or regulate U.S. businesses, this site can save you a lot of time. The searchable FAQs include information from all these organizations, and the site provides access to state and local information as well. Everything from paying taxes and financing a business to selling your goods and services to the government is covered here.

Internal Revenue Service (IRS)
www.irs.gov/businesses/small/

When you become self-employed or open a business, the complexity of your taxes can change dramatically. The IRS's business center includes a section devoted to small businesses and the self-employed. It should be one of your first stops as you begin to plan. View a streaming video of an IRS small-business workshop, take an IRS course, or complete an online self-directed version of a workshop taught live around the country. Or find downloadable forms and publications, learn about electronic filing, browse small-business news stories and tax-law changes, and more.

SCORE: Counselors to America's Small Business

www.score.org

The 10,500 members of SCORE, the Service Corps of Retired Executives, provide free and confidential e-mail and in-person small-business mentoring and advice. Use this site to locate an office near you, or search for an e-mail counselor whose skills match your needs. You'll also find success stories, articles, information and links on starting a business, free planning workbooks, and free e-mail newsletters on resources and entrepreneurial issues. Having helped over 8 million small businesses since 1964, there's no reason not to pay a visit.

Small Business Watchdog

http://weblog.sba.gov/blog-advo/

According to this blog, there are roughly 27 million small businesses in the United States. If you are thinking about entrepreneurship, you are part of an enormous and steadily growing group with its own special interests. The Small Business Watchdog makes its mission to encourage policies that help small businesses succeed. For that reason alone, it can be useful to visit this blog and learn what policies and trends are affecting the small business industry. While not exactly geared toward the freelancer with an employee base of one, this site is useful for any small business owner who faces regulations of any sort and wants to know how his or her business will be affected by policy changes and current economic trends.

State and Local Government on the Net

www.statelocalgov.net

Don't forget to check with state and local agencies for business regulations and requirements in your location. Fortunately, this handy directory helps you find those agencies in a few clicks. For most states, look for the department of commerce under the executive branch listings.

U.S. Small Business Administration (SBA)

www.sbaonline.sba.gov

The SBA is one of your best stops on the road to self-employment. Plan to visit often—there's too much to grasp in one visit. Start with the Small Business Planner, which includes detailed information on starting and managing your business. You can also check out the Services tab for free online courses; applications for registrations, licences, and financial assistance; and more. Locate your local office, browse FAQs for answers to the questions that aspiring small-business owners most often ask, and find detailed information on common tasks such as creating your business plan. Other features include online chats, podcasts, an e-newsletter, and information on training opportunities. This site is also available in Spanish.

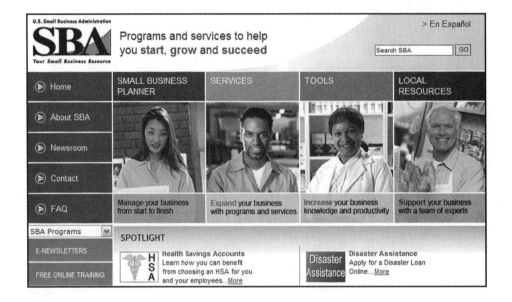

Small-Business Solutions

The Web sites in this section provide a mix of information and services for new and experienced entrepreneurs. Start-up business owners will appreciate the getting-started information about writing business plans and the like. Experienced entrepreneurs looking for new business trends, new marketing channels, or just new ideas won't be disappointed either.

About.com: Small Business Information

http://sbinformation.about.com

Although About.com is unfortunately heavy on distracting advertising, this site offers extensive information for small-business owners (and aspiring owners). Subscribe to a free e-mail newsletter, join the discussion forum, read featured articles, learn about business blogging, or select a topic of interest from the subject links here. Each subject link contains a number of links to useful sites on the topic. Subjects range from writing business plans to economic trends.

AllBusiness.com

www.allbusiness.com

> With how-to articles, business forms, contracts and agreements, expert advice, blogs, business news, business directory listings, product comparisons, business guides, and more, AllBusiness.com just might become your go-to site for business questions. Topics here range from business plans, consulting, and incorporating to personal finance, sales and marketing, and technology. In addition, free registration gives you full access to the AllBusiness.com periodicals library of more than 700,000 articles from 400 leading business and industry publications plus a choice of free subscriptions to e-newsletters. You can browse the site multiple ways, by business advice category, by industry, by most popular, or by using its search engine. And if you are thinking about starting a franchise, AllBusiness offers a franchise finder as well.

Bplans.com

www.bplans.com

> You need a business plan before you can get financing for your new business—not to mention the need to clarify your plans and prospects before starting. Learn by example at Bplans.com, which provides 100+ sample business plans for free online viewing (they have many more, but you have to pay for those). Other freebies here include interactive tools to walk you through calculating starting costs, finding financing options, and creating an initial assessment for your business plan. The site also includes expert answers to questions on business and marketing plans, planning software and entrepreneurship, and articles on starting and managing a business.

Business Owners' Idea Café

www.businessownersideacafe.com

> For "a fun approach to serious business," visit the Business Owners' Idea Café. Interact with other entrepreneurs and experts in the Cyberschmooz area, and find tons of resources for starting and running a small business. Free registration gives you access to the small-business grant center,

newsletter, contests, opportunities to promote your business, and more. Although the approach might be casual, the advice is anything but. You'll find a lot of useful information in a quick and friendly format, not to mention lots of people who will empathize with your struggles to start your own business.

CCH Business Owner's Toolkit

www.toolkit.com

The Toolkit offers a great deal of useful information and tools to let you start and run your own successful business, from experts who know their stuff. Scroll down to see the different categories in the small-business guide, ranging from writing a business plan to hiring the right people. You'll also find free downloadable business tools, including sample policies and forms that you can use and/or modify for your own purposes. Also check out the Ask Alice! advice column for Q&A on small-business issues. The Toolkit is a free service of CCH Tax and Accounting, a provider of business, legal, and tax information and software.

GoDaddy

www.godaddy.com/

At first glance, GoDaddy doesn't look like a site geared toward helping the self-employed make their dreams come true. Unless your dream is to start your own Internet-based business. If that's the case, then GoDaddy has a buffet of valuable tools at your disposal. Here you can purchase domain names, build and host your Web site, set up business-based e-mail accounts, and market your business on the Internet. None of this comes free, of course, but GoDaddy's costs are comparable and the range of services extensive. It's certainly worth checking out if you know you want to sell and market yourself over the Web but aren't quite sure how to get started.

How to Start a Small Business

http://sbdc.deltacollege.org/startup/

An online book and award-winning Web site in one, this site from the San Joaquin Delta College Small Business Development Center is full of information and resources on starting your own business. Start with the table of contents to get a breakdown of the topics covered here, or read straight through for complete coverage of all the steps involved. Each section includes links to additional articles, information, and sites. An interactive index allows you to locate the specific information you need with just a click. Even better, there are no ads, and no registration is required for full site access. This site is also available in Spanish.

International Virtual Assistants Association

www.ivaa.org/

To know if this Web site will be valuable to you, you first need to know if you are a Virtual Assistant. According to the IVAA, a virtual assistant is "an independent entrepreneur providing administrative, creative and/or technical services." In short, a VA is an expert who works on a contractual basis, primarily by telecommuting, and the IVAA supports those in the industry by providing networking, a mentorship program, free Web site hosting, scholarships, certifications, marketing assistance, and more. If you think you are a VA, or think you might want to become one, this is a good site to check out. Alternatively, if you are a small business who needs to farm out some work, you can contact the IVAA and have them put you in touch with professional assistants who can meet your needs.

Network Solutions

www.networksolutions.com

> Thinking about getting your own domain name for a Web site? Find
> out if your first choice is available by searching the database at Network
> Solutions. The granddaddy of domain registrars, Network Solutions is now
> only one of many domain name registration services. For more (and often
> cheaper) options, see the Accredited Registrar Directory from ICANN, the
> Internet Corporation for Assigned Names and Numbers, at www.
> internic.net/regist.html.

Nolo.com

www.nolo.com

> Nolo is the name for legal information for the busy small-business owner
> on a budget, whether you're dealing with business and human resources;
> patents, copyright, and art; wills and estate planning; property and money;
> family law and immigration; or rights and disputes. Read articles, get
> advice, and use action step checklists or interactive calculators. You can
> also locate and purchase helpful do-it-yourself legal titles and software
> from Nolo if you need further information or print references. Some
> background reading here may provide what you need or help you fine-tune
> your questions to take to your clock-watching attorney.

Operating Your Successful Small Business

http://sbdc.deltacollege.org/inbusiness/

> Here's another online book from the San Joaquin Delta College Small
> Business Development Center. This one's about keeping your business
> afloat and on course after a successful launch. Browse the table of con-
> tents for topics of interest, or find specific information through the index.
> A list of other online resources is organized into categories such as com-
> mercial enterprises, directories, employees, government contracting, and
> inventions. As with How to Start a Business (discussed earlier in this sec-
> tion), you see no ads, and you don't register for access to the information.

Franchises

Franchises provide a ready-made business opportunity for those who want to start their own business with the security of an established brand behind their efforts. The sites in this section cover places to find franchise opportunities and discuss franchising in general.

BISON: The Franchise Network

www.bison.com

> If you're thinking of buying a franchise, BISON can steer you in some helpful directions. BISON (for Business International Sales and Opportunity Network) strives to provide comprehensive information on franchising, so there is a lot to explore here. Search here for franchise opportunities by subject, and find information on each company, including costs. Each includes a link to request more information (but note that your net worth and liquid capital are required). You'll also find franchising news, profiles of featured franchises, and financing options.

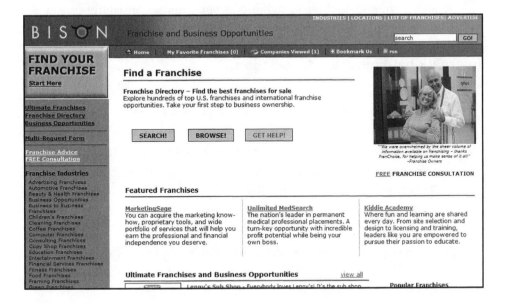

Entrepreneur.com Franchise Zone

www.entrepreneur.com/franchiseopportunities/index.html

On this portal for franchisers, you'll find news, advice, articles, and assistance. The franchise directory contains categorized opportunities, as well as lists of the top global, low-cost, fastest-growing, and new franchises. The information on each company includes investment requirements, fees, and funding information; background and contact information; information on franchise growth; where the company stands in *Entrepreneur* magazine's franchise rankings; the type of training and support the company provides; and suggestions on where it is seeking franchisees. Also check out the Franchise Zone for articles, tips, and how-tos.

Franchising.com

www.franchising.com

Is franchising for you? At Franchising.com you can learn how to make the franchising decision, be a successful franchisee, and find the franchise opportunity that's right for you. The site provides detailed information about various franchising and business opportunities, insightful articles, a directory of franchise attorneys, and other franchising resources.

International Franchise Association

www.franchise.org/

The site is broken into three separate categories. Using the "Own a Franchise" tools, you can discover and research more than 1,200 franchise opportunities around the globe. You can also get help acquiring a franchise or contact a franchise consultant to walk you through the process. By becoming a member of the IFA, you get access to even more resources, including a database of suppliers, using the Franchise Community. Finally, if you are new to franchising or simply want to learn more about the opportunities available, check out Franchising Basics for an introduction to franchising and all the latest news and information. Membership in IFA is available for franchisors, franchisees, and suppliers.

Online Business Magazines

The energy is high at these online business magazines. Online publications make keeping "in the know" quick and convenient. And with the searchable magazine archives, there's no longer a need for you to keep back issues.

CNNMoney.com

http://money.cnn.com/

CNNMoney.com is the Internet home for two of the most popular business and financial magazines: *Fortune* and *Money*. You can read the entire contents of the magazines—including back issues—for free online, or you can search one or all for specific words or phrases. No registration is required unless you want to subscribe to an e-newsletter, and there are several to choose from.

Entrepreneur.com

www.entrepreneur.com

Anything you could want to know about small business you can probably find here, either by browsing the 14 categories or conducting a keyword search. Upper-level topics include Starting a Business, Money, Marketing, Sales, Advertising, Franchises, Biz Opportunities, Home Based Biz, E-Business, and more. Each is full of articles, how-tos, success stories, and lots of ideas and advice. If that's not enough, you can read the current and past issues of *Entrepreneur* magazine.

Fast Company

www.fastcompany.com

> *Fast Company* wants to be the first word in cutting-edge business thinking, and the magazine has made waves since its launch in 1997. The Web site's content is generous, with every article in every issue (except the current issue) archived online, searchable, and conveniently organized by topic. Fast Company Online Guides are editor-selected collections of the best articles on the Internet and technology, leadership, marketing and branding, sales and customer service, strategy and innovation, and more. If you like blogs, you can read not only FC Now, the *Fast Company* blog, but also choose from more than 50 others. Registration is free.

Inc.com

www.inc.com

> Pitched as "The Daily Resource for Entrepreneurs," Inc.com's robust but busy homepage features resource centers (organized by topic), blogs, feature stories, access to newsletters, and videos on Inc.TV. Browse through Inc.com's collection of articles organized by topics such as finance and capital, technology, leadership, e-commerce, law and taxation, and much more. Check out the current issue's table of contents, or get lots of how-to advice on everything from finding and retaining customers to gearing

up for tax time. With a free Inc.com membership, you get access to more than 100 free tools, such as interactive worksheets and a choice of free e-mail newsletters.

Business Associations

Business associations are a great place to network with other small-business owners, get ideas, find resources, and build new business opportunities. This section contains some Web sites of general associations to get you started. Also consider associations focusing on your business's specialty.

National Association for the Self-Employed (NASE)

www.nase.org

> NASE focuses exclusively on the needs of "micro-businesses"—those with no more than 10 employees. NASE aims to help members tackle issues such as business financing and affordable health care through providing how-to resources, access to a wide range of professional services at discounted rates, and legislative advocacy. NASE members have access to a number of tools and programs, but anyone can browse the micro-business topics or download advice from NASE experts.

National Federation of Independent Business (NFIB)

www.nfib.com

> NFIB is a large advocacy organization for small business, with a membership of more than 600,000 businesses. Learn about state and national issues facing small-business owners, search the database of business articles for practical information and tips for small-business owners, and find out about member benefits. Member benefits are similar to those for NASE, including health, travel, service, and other discounts.

U.S. Chamber of Commerce

www.uschamber.com

>As you establish your small business, consider taking advantage of the ser-
>vices of your local Chamber of Commerce. Chambers provide members
>with invaluable networking opportunities, business contacts, and busi-
>ness education options. Click on the Chambers tab to locate your local
>Chamber and to link directly to its Web site (when available) for more
>information. The U.S. Chamber of Commerce site also includes news,
>events, member benefits, and advocacy information.

SOHO: Small Office/Home Office

Almost 20 million Americans now work at least one day a week from home, either
through a telecommuting/freelance arrangement with outside employers or in their
own home-based business. The work-at-home trend continues so strongly that
it's become a market segment with its own catchy acronym: SOHO (small office/
home office). The Web sites in this section cover the work-at-home lifestyle in
general. For information on telecommuting, contracting, and freelancing, see
chapter 8.

A Home-Based Business Online (AHBBO)

www.ahbbo.com

> If you're hunting for a home-based business idea, check out the master
> list of ideas at AHBBO. Detailed information on 130 businesses is also
> available for download for a fee. Subscribe to the AHBBO e-zine and
> get caught up by reading the archives of past issues. Be sure to check out
> the article library, which is loaded with home-based business information
> ranging from how to successfully market your business to how to avoid
> schemes and frauds.

Home Based Businesses: Business.gov

www.business.gov/guides/home-based/

> From the very first site discussed in this chapter comes this specialized
> portal for people starting a home-based business. The resources here are
> clearly organized and walk you through the steps of creating and managing
> your business from your study. Learn how to market your business, cre-
> ate a business plan, buy a work-at-home franchise, and plan for taxes, or
> check out the Virtual Resource Library for tools to get you started.

Work-at-Home.Org

www.work-at-home.org

> There are lots of reasons you might consider working from home: to raise
> a family, to help the environment, to gain a measure of independence,
> or simply to do your work in your pajamas. Regardless of the motive,
> Work-at-Home.org can help by providing work-at-home job opportunities
> (scam-free), articles and advice on how to manage the unique pressures of
> the WAH lifestyle, and links to other helpful resources. The site isn't well
> organized—you may have to click around to find what you want—but the
> people behind the site are passionate about supporting others who strive
> to balance their career and life by choosing to work from the office next
> to their living room rather than the one down the street.

Working Solo

www.workingsolo.com

> Working Solo extends a helping hand to the solo self-employed by pro-
> viding a free monthly e-newsletter, FAQs about starting a solo business,

and SOHO resources and articles. This Web site is the companion to the *Working Solo* series of books by best-selling SOHO author Terri Lonier.

Resources for Women Business Owners

Following are some valuable resources for up-and-coming women who own businesses—both large and small—and work at home.

SBA-Sponsored

Online Women's Business Center (OWBC)
www.onlinewbc.gov

The U.S. has more than 10 million woman-owned businesses, and the U.S. Small Business Administration (SBA) Office of Women's Business Ownership sponsors the OWBC to help them (and newer startups) succeed. Links take you to the SBA's resources on starting, financing, and managing a business (see U.S. Small Business Administration, discussed in the first section). SBA representatives specially trained in assisting female entrepreneurs are available in every SBA regional office, and you can locate the one nearest you through this Web site. The SBA Women's Business Center Program provides a network of more than 100 educational resource centers across the country—all listed here. Check out the resources page to learn about mentoring programs, find answers to frequently asked questions, and get motivated by inspiring success stories. This site is also available in Spanish.

Other Resources Mainly for Women

Christian Work at Home Moms Blog
http://cwahm.com/wordpress/

> Christian Work at Home Moms provides job listings, information, resources, and spiritual encouragement to Christian parents (moms and dads) who want to work at home. You can also find articles, work-at-home ideas, advertising opportunities, and podcasts here, and CWAHM provides networking opportunities with other Christian parents. While the site is geared toward those of the Christian faith, anyone who wants to learn more about work-at-home opportunities or look for specific jobs can find what they are looking for here.

Internet Based Moms
www.internetbasedmoms.com

> The Internet offers business opportunities your mother never had, and you can learn the ins and outs of an Internet-based business at Internet Based Moms. From advice on choosing and starting an Internet business to building an income-producing Web site to optimizing search engine results to promoting your business online, you'll find it here. Membership is free and gives you access to the busy discussion boards, the weekly e-newsletter, and the online chat rooms, as well as other resources. You can even check out the Just for Moms section for tips on money and savings, time management, health and well being, and even recipes.

Jobs and Moms Career Center
www.jobsandmoms.com

> This nicely laid-out site features many options for work-at-home moms, from starting your own business to buying a franchise, engaging in direct sales or working for an employer. In addition to specific opportunities, site author Nancy Collamer lists additional resources such as government agencies, books, and professional associations. The full-feature job board can help you locate employers who are actively recruiting work-at-home professionals. Free subscription to the newsletter also includes a free copy of Collamer's e-book, *You Can Do It! 25 Powerful (and Free) Resources to Help Jumpstart Your Mom-Friendly Career.*

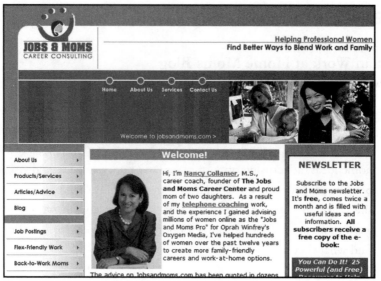

National Association for Female Executives (NAFE)

www.nafe.com

> More than 60,000 strong, NAFE is the largest women's association for professionals and business owners in the U.S. NAFE supports its members with networking opportunities, education, and public advocacy. In addition, member benefits include discounts on many personal and business services such as insurance, banking, technology, and more.

National Association of Women Business Owners (NAWBO)

www.nawbo.org

> Most of the content at this Web site is accessible only to members, but if you are a business owner, it might be worth it. Like the business associations discussed earlier in this chapter, NAWBO provides member benefits such as corporate and insurance discounts and other services through a business resource center. Members' profiles are available in a searchable Web directory for easy networking with other women business owners. This site is also available in Spanish.

WAHM.com: Work at Home Moms

www.wahm.com

> WAHM.com is an online magazine for work-at-home moms, a sector of the labor force with unique needs and concerns. Even the name sounds

like a crying kid. But that may be intentional, judging from the generous humor dished up at this site, not to mention a ton of resources in a friend-ly format. These include a free weekly e-mail newsletter, telecommuting job listings, active online forums, work-at-home ideas, business opportuni-ties, recipes, a directory of WAHMs near you, and more. Promote your business by adding information to the online WAHM directory, and don't forget to enjoy the weekly cartoon.

Work It, Mom! Blog

www.workitmom.com/blog

Work it, Mom! Is the place "where working moms connect." As such, the most valuable feature of this Web site are the blogs and discussion boards where those working moms come together to discuss the ins and outs of balancing work and home life. Though not specifically geared toward female entrepreneurs, the articles, advice, tips, and resources you find here will be useful to anyone who has struggles to juggle career and family. Using the categories at the top, you can hone in on subjects that concern you most. Women business owners will find the information and advice listed under "Your Business" especially useful. And what site concerned with balancing work and home life would be complete without a Quick Recipe section?

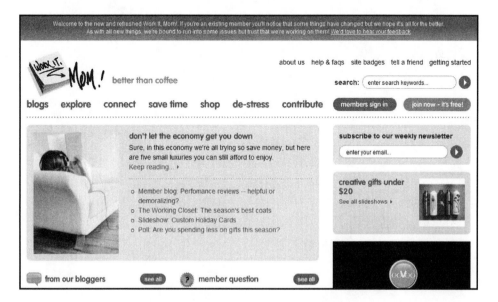

Women for Hire Blog

http://blog.womenforhire.com/

> With more than 30,000 members, Women For Hire is one of the fastest-growing organizations for women workers. The organization started by hosting career expos where top employers would meet with talented female professionals. The company grew from there to include books, a magazine, and the above comprehensive Web site. From this site, you can get advice on all aspects of your career, search the Women For Hire job board, access resume and cover letter templates, join a professional network of women workers, and learn about work-from-home opportunities. If you need a pick-me-up, get inspiration from the "Be Gutsy Blog."

WomanOwned.com

www.womanowned.com

> If you're interested in starting or growing a business, you'll find some good reading here. Articles range from brainstorming for ideas to recruiting and developing an advisory board. Through the membership-based business portal, you can find and network with other woman-owned businesses and continue your networking efforts in online forums, as well as access other services and benefits.

Temporary Work, Contract Employment, Freelancing, Teleworking, and Volunteering

You have more possibilities than ever these days when it comes to working. The value and benefit of temporary jobs, freelance work, contract work, and telecommuting are getting more recognition as these alternatives to 9-to-5 work are becoming more common.

Employers can pay more for contracted or temporary work to meet specific needs or peak business activities and still save on employment costs in the long run. Individuals can use temporary or contract work to transition between jobs, gain job experience, break into a new field, avoid boredom, control their work schedules, and (often) make more money.

Then there's working for no money. The U.S. has a strong tradition of volunteer work, from the grassroots level up to nationwide. Volunteer work can pay rewards that can't be measured in dollars and cents. Whether you take on flexible work that pays well or not at all, each can provide valuable experience and can open your eyes to new careers and possibilities.

General Information on Temporary Work, Contract Employment, and Freelancing

The line between being employed or self-employed gets blurred around temp work, contract employment, and freelancing. Temps usually work for and are paid by an agency that finds positions for them and places them in various settings. Contractors may work for such an agency, may be traditionally self-employed, or may contract with an organization that functions as their "employer" while they retain full autonomy over their work (such as PACE, described in this section). Freelancers are typically self-employed in creative professions—designers, writers, artists—although they may also choose a different business model to meet their needs.

One of these needs is employment benefits, especially health insurance. If you're considering an alternative to traditional full-time employment, be sure to figure in the cost of self-paid employment benefits. Fortunately, there are viable options for you here as well, and these sites will give you leads.

AllFreelance.com Freelance Jobs Directory

www.allfreelance.com

> Anything freelance can be found through this directory. This hefty collection of freelance-related links is organized into topics: freelance job sites, freelance articles, work-at-home job sites, telecommuting jobs, online courses, project management, weekly articles, message boards, and more. This site can help you to figure your taxes, network with other freelancers, find insurance, and better promote yourself. Lots of reading and resources will keep you coming back.

The Contract Employee's Handbook

www.cehandbook.com

> The Contract Employee's Handbook is a great help if you're interested in or working as a skilled temporary employee. Contract employees, sometimes referred to as leased employees, are employed by a contract employment agency and assigned to work in client companies. Learn here about the types of contract employment agencies, the types of contractors, how

to work the system to your advantage, legal matters, and more. You also can sign up for a free biweekly e-mail newsletter for professional and technical contractors.

freelancemom.com

www.freelancemom.com

While not *quite* as general as the other sites in this section, freelancemom provides accessible, down-to-earth advice for professional moms who want to work from home. Check out the blogs, read the featured articles, contribute to the discussions in the forums, or check out the resources section for information on how to build a Web site, find a freelance gig, or create a WAHM (work at home mom) business idea. You can also register for free to receive the monthly newsletter.

Freelance Switch

www.freelanceswitch.com

Freelance Switch is the online equivalent of a freelancer's coffeehouse. Peruse the blog, listen to podcasts, or join the forums to learn the latest trends in freelancing. Check out the resources section for a rates calculator, client analyzer, or the "Guide to Passive Income." The Job Board provides a list of openings, though you will need a paid subscription to Freelance Switch in order to apply.

Professional Association for Contract Employment (PACE)

www.pacepros.com

> PACE offers a new business model for contract professionals, whether you work independently or for a contracting agency. Through PACE, you can retain all the independence and tax advantages of being a self-employed contract professional, but PACE is your official employer of record for tax purposes, simulating a one-person corporation. PACE can also provide "back office" services such as online timesheets, invoicing, and payroll processing with direct deposit, as well as group benefits and career-support services. PACE is not a recruiting agency, but future plans call for developing a marketing center to help contract professionals market their services directly to prospective clients. The executive director of PACE is James R. Ziegler, Ph.D., author of The Contract Employee's Handbook, just described.

Work Sources for Temporary Work, Contract Employment, and Freelancing

Explore all your alternatives at these sites, which present a variety of opportunities and employment arrangements for you to consider.

Aquent

www.aquent.com

> Aquent works like an agent for creative and IT professionals, helping them find projects, temp work, and full-time employment. Fill out an online application to see whether Aquent will represent you. If you are hired through Aquent, it handles billing and the other details involved in contract work and makes other benefits available, such as health, dental, and workers compensation insurance and 401(k) plans.

Creative Freelancers

www.freelancers1.com

Freelance designers, illustrators, writers, editors, photographers, Web designers, and other creative types can get Internet exposure through Creative Freelancers. Enter your free profile into the database and show up in talent searches conducted by both Creative Freelancers and outside employers. Value-added information includes a pricing guide, legal help, and links to clubs, organizations, and other resources for creative professionals.

Elance

www.elance.com

Elance Marketplace, a fee-based site, connects companies that have outsourcing needs with professionals who can provide those services. Service providers have a choice of different subscriptions, ranging from a free courtesy listing to a select professional package. Choose the monthly, quarterly, or yearly option, or subscribe by category to see only listings appropriate to your industry. Extensive tips guide you through the process, and sample letters and agreements are available for free.

Kelly Services

www.kellyservices.us

Kelly Services, the oldest name in temp agencies, provides employees in a variety of fields to companies around the globe. Search for contract and regular opportunities by location, category, or keyword. Check out Kelly's salary surveys, career assessment tools, book recommendations, articles, and more.

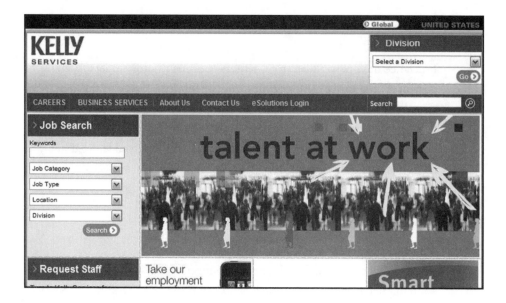

Manpower
www.manpower.com

> One of the biggest providers of staffing services with 4,500 offices world-
> wide, Manpower provides a searchable database of current opportunities,
> a list of local offices, and information on why you might want to work for
> Manpower. This site is also available in French and Spanish.

MediaBistro
www.mediabistro.com

> MediaBistro started as an after-hours social gathering for creative profes-
> sionals and quickly turned into a multidimensional Web site designed to
> help people working in content/creative industries. Here people who work
> with books, television, film, radio, online media, advertising, and other
> design-related fields can come together to share their work and ideas, find
> business opportunities, and catch up on news and trends. Features include
> a job board, online courses, seminars, "learn" e-mails, and media industry
> blogs. Of particular interest to freelancers is the Freelance Marketplace,
> where freelancers create profiles that showcase their work so that employ-
> ers can find them easily. Finally, there's always a party to be found on
> MediaBistro…although you have to ask to be invited.

Net-Temps

www.net-temps.com

> Net-Temps specializes in job postings for the staffing industry, includ-
> ing temporary, temporary-to-permanent, and full-time positions. You can
> search the job listings by location and keyword or browse by category.
> You can also register to post your resume online (from Microsoft Word or
> using the resume builder tool), use job search agents, and receive postings
> via e-mail—all for free. When registering or searching, specify whether
> you'd like just contract positions or both contract and direct-hire opportu-
> nities. You can apply online for most positions. You can also read a num-
> ber of career development articles and get advice on changing careers.

Freelancers Union

www.freelancersunion.org

> Independent workers—freelancers, consultants, independent contrac-
> tors, temps, part-timers, contingent employees, and the self-employed—
> make up about 30% of the nation's workforce. As a national nonprofit,
> Freelancers Union's goal is to support America's growing independent
> workforce through advocacy, information, and service. Join for a modest
> yearly fee to receive member discounts on legal and dental services, office
> products, and other items useful to the independent worker. An additional
> one-time setup fee provides access to group health insurance. Browse
> through helpful resources and articles for further information on topics
> such as benefits issues and finances.

Teleworking/Telecommuting

The most recent statistics from the U.S. Census Bureau report that nearly 20 million Americans work at least one day a week at home, either for themselves or for
an employer. Cell phones, low-priced desktop and laptop computers, fax, e-mail,
PDAs, and other technology allow telecommuters to keep in constant contact from
home or anywhere. Challenges exist, however, such as managing your time effectively and controlling your barking dog when you're on the phone. Telecommuting
is often an arrangement you make with your employer, although some companies
now recruit specifically for telecommuting jobs. In addition to this section, see

the "SOHO: Small Office/Home Office" and "Resources for Women Business Owners" sections in chapter 7.

Better Business Bureau: Work-at-Home Schemes
http://us.bbb.org

> Get savvy about work-at-home opportunities. A lot of valid ones exist, but, unfortunately, so do work-at-home scams. Falling for one is double trouble. Not only can you lose money, time, and your reputation, but you can be held liable for perpetrating a fraud, even unintentionally. Fortunately, the Better Business Bureau provides information on how to recognize and avoid being taken by phony work-at-home schemes, including a list of the most common scams and sample job ads to avoid. To get there, start with the BBB home page and click on the For Consumers tab. From there go to the Resource Library and click on FTC Articles for Consumers. There you'll find a link to Investment and Business Opportunities, which includes information on franchise opportunities, investment schemes, and work-at-home schemes. The best advice? If it sounds too good to be true, it probably is.

HomeworkersNet
www.homeworkersnet.com

> Sign up for the free e-mail newsletter that lists work-at-home job opportunities that aren't posted online. Then go on to explore the rest of the site, including a job listings section that pulls work-at-home opportunities from a number of job banks. Each opening is researched by HomeworkersNet to help you avoid less-than-legitimate offers. Check back often for daily featured positions. Other sections include a directory of other sites devoted to home-based employment, an employer directory, home business ideas, and articles and advice.

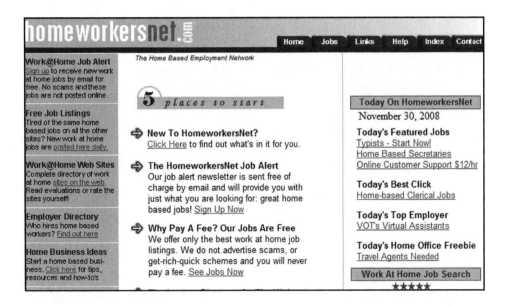

InnoVisions Canada/Canadian Telework Association

www.ivc.ca

> InnoVisions Canada and the nonprofit Canadian Telework Association
> team up here to provide a ton of worldwide information, statistics, and
> resources on telecommuting. Find out about everything from telecommut-
> ing and disabilities to conferences and taxes—and everything in between.

Jobs and Moms

www.jobsandmoms.com/

> This site was founded by career coach Nancy Collamer and offers advice
> for professional-level women looking for flexible jobs, work-at-home
> opportunities, and innovative work/life resources. Here you can find job
> opportunities, read advice on how to find and manage "flex-friendly"
> work, catch up on the latest trends, or order the "Back to Work Toolkit."
> Two of the more interesting resources are the "Home-Based Business Idea
> Generator" and the "Mom's Biz Showcase," which highlights success-
> ful businesses started by work-at-home moms and dads. For those with a
> really busy home life, there's the "Work-Life Goodies" section containing
> links to services for babysitting, nannies, restaurant coupons, and more.

Telecommuting Jobs

www.tjobs.com

> View free job listings in categories including artists, programmers, writers, web designers, data entry, and engineers. A low-cost membership lets you respond to job postings and post your resume online to show up in talent searches by employers. You can also create a low-cost "InSiteOffice" page that shows you mean business with a professional at-home setup. Other helpful sections include free articles and statistics, as well as links to certification, training, and other useful resources for telecommuters.

Telework Coalition

www.telcoa.org

> The Telework Coalition (TelCoa) is a nonprofit organization promoting the economic, social, and environmental benefits of telecommuting. Join to get access to research reports and discounts on products and services, or just browse through the free information on this site for conference dates, articles, quick facts, and related links.

YouCanWorkFromAnywhere.com

www.youcanworkfromanywhere.com

> Telecommuters, mobile workers, road warriors, and home-based workers can find tips, articles, classes, e-books, newsletters, and more on working effectively in nontraditional ways. Find out how to use technology effectively while telecommuting, such as by locating Wi-Fi (wireless technology) hotspots to get online. This comprehensive site is a great place to find information on getting started as a telecommuter and working more effectively from home.

Volunteer Opportunities

Have you looked at volunteering lately? There's executive volunteering, mid-career volunteering, volunteering vacations, volunteer matching, and virtual volunteering. Volunteering "jobs" range from one week (at Global Volunteers, described in this section) to the 27 months required by the Peace Corps (also described in this section). Volunteering can give you valuable experience for your resume and the intangible benefit of making a difference in the world.

1-800-Volunteer.org

www.1-800-volunteer.org

> 1-800-Volunteer.org is "America's Address for Volunteering." Here you can get connected to volunteer opportunities in your community (or anywhere your talents are needed), track your volunteer service, and receive automatic e-mail notifications when you're needed most. Find a volunteer opportunity by searching by issue area or ZIP code (there are more than 26,000 to choose from). If no opportunities exist in your area, no problem—the organization also lists virtual volunteer jobs that you can do from home. This site also is available in Spanish.

American Red Cross

www.redcross.org/services/volunteer/

> If you feel the urge to help out but giving blood makes you squeamish, check the American Red Cross's Web site for other volunteer opportunities. In addition to its blood bank, the American Red Cross is well-known for its disaster relief services, health and safety skills training, and more. Read all about it at this Web site, including articles and inspirational stories from volunteers. Locate your local chapter by ZIP code.

Citizens Development Corps

www.cdc.org

> The Citizens Development Corps is devoted to economic development in emerging and transitioning economies worldwide through the use of experienced business professionals. A network of more than 7,000 expert volunteer advisors from every industry and skill set provides programs dealing with association building, export promotion, job creation, policy and regulatory reform, privatization, procurement and supplier training, and more. Learn about the benefits of volunteering and the participation requirements, and browse the currently open assignments.

Corporation for National & Community Service

www.cns.gov

> This federally funded site offers three major opportunities for public service. Through AmeriCorps, volunteers devote a year to giving back to the community through educational, environmental, health, and public safety services. Senior Corps taps the skills of older citizens through foster grandparents, senior companions, and other volunteer opportunities. Learn and Serve America lets the younger generation combine volunteerism with education through their schools. Find out about these programs, search for other volunteer opportunities, or connect with other members or service alums.

Global Volunteers

www.globalvolunteers.org

> Take a different kind of vacation by volunteering abroad or in the U.S. in community development projects that last one to three weeks. Service

projects with Global Volunteers range from tutoring and teaching English to childcare, construction, and healthcare. No specialized skills are required. Find out whether the program is right for you by reading the FAQs, checking out different service programs, or subscribing to the e-newsletter.

Idealist

www.idealist.org

Mentioned briefly in chapter 4, Idealist brings together nonprofit organizations, nonprofit professionals, and volunteers with a searchable database of opportunities. Sign up to have new work or volunteer opportunities e-mailed to you and to have your skills listed in the database so that organizations can easily find you. Other neat ideas here include volunteering with your family, volunteering abroad, and making a career out of nonprofit work by searching Idealist's career center for jobs and internships with these organizations. You can also search for or browse organizations by area of interest or geographic location to find out who is doing what and participate in online discussion groups. This site also is available in Spanish and French.

International Executive Service Corps (IESC)
www.iesc.org

> IESC is a professional economic development organization that uses volunteer experts, professional staff, and strategic partners. It provides a wide range of services, such as technical, managerial, and professional consulting; trade and investment services; small grants administration; training programs; international standards certification; and more. Funded primarily through the U.S. Agency for International Development, IESC operates in more than 60 countries. Read the FAQs, or, better yet, read the firsthand accounts of IESC volunteers, and then register online if you meet the qualifications.

Peace Corps
www.peacecorps.gov

> Find out about recruiting events, e-mail or find a recruiter, or apply online to serve overseas as a Peace Corps volunteer. The Peace Corps needs volunteers in areas such as education, information technology, agriculture, health, environment, business, and community development. Read through stories from volunteers to find out what volunteering abroad is really like, read news stories, and find out about other benefits such as student loan deferment, job placement, and training services for returned volunteers. Kids can even become virtual volunteers by taking the fun online Peace Corps Challenge. This site also is available in French and Spanish.

Points of Light Foundation
www.pointsoflight.org

> The Points of Light Foundation was organized in 1990 for the purpose of engaging more people more effectively in volunteer community service to help solve serious social problems. Here you can locate your local Points of Light volunteer center, find out about the foundation mission and programs, and access other resources. The Points of Light Foundation and the Volunteer Center National Network Council collaboratively sponsor 1-800-Volunteer.org (described earlier in this section).

SERVEnet

http://servenet.org

> SERVEnet is a free matching service for volunteers and organizations. Either do a quick search by ZIP code to list organizations and opportunities in your area, or use the advanced search to more closely match your skills to available opportunities. You can find out about special volunteer events across the nation, virtual (online) volunteer opportunities, and how to be a successful volunteer. If you register and create a profile, local nonprofits can notify you about volunteer opportunities that match your skills, interests, and schedule. SERVEnet is a program of Youth Service America.

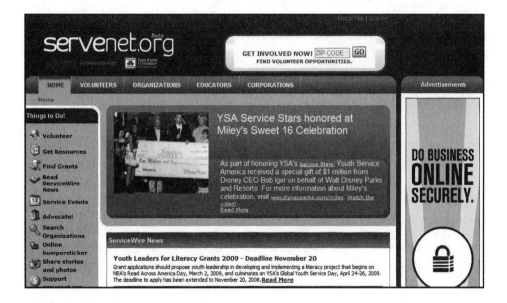

Teach For America

www.teachforamerica.org

> New and recent college graduates with a desire to teach and a sense of adventure will want to check out this Web site. Teach For America is a public service program that places trained corps members in schools that have a critical need for qualified, certified teachers. The program accepts students from many academic disciplines, not just education. Successful program applicants complete an intensive five-week residential summer institute before getting their two-year assignments. Subscribe to the free

applicant newsletter, fill out an online application, and find out more about the program at this Web site.

United Nations Volunteers

www.unv.org

Each year, nearly 7,500 volunteers from more than 150 countries contribute their efforts to the United Nations Volunteers program, which works through United Nations Development Programme offices around the world. Learn about the recruitment process for volunteering abroad, and find out how to apply to volunteer at home, abroad, or even online. For inspiration, read about the experiences of UN volunteers working for peace and development around the globe.

Volunteer.gov

www.volunteer.gov/gov/

As a partnership among several departments of the federal government, including the Corporation for National and Community Service and the U.S.A. Freedom Corps, Volunteer.gov aims to be an easy-to-use portal for volunteer opportunities. Search by state, activity, keyword, or date, or just click on "Newest Opportunities" if you are a regular visitor.

VolunteerMatch

www.volunteermatch.org

As the name suggests, VolunteerMatch provides a free matching service for volunteers and organizations. Put in your ZIP code to find places to volunteer in your area, or choose the virtual volunteering option and browse through ways to contribute your skills without leaving home. This Web site also lets you create a personal volunteer account to receive personalized e-mails and manage your online volunteer resume. Get inspired reading the volunteer stories showcased each month.

Volunteer Solutions

www.volunteersolutions.org

Nothing complicated here. If you are looking for a volunteer opportunity, simply type your ZIP code on the bare-bones homepage and start browsing. If you find something you like, use the site's handy form to e-mail the contact person. Although this site may not be the most informative, there's no denying its ease-of-use.

Volunteer-Related Associations

If you're interested in a career either with a nonprofit or in the field of volunteerism, these associations may give you some ideas to pursue.

Alliance for Nonprofit Management

www.allianceonline.org

> The Alliance for Nonprofit Management is devoted to the management and government of nonprofit organizations. Its Resource Center is an annotated, searchable database of organizations, Web sites, books, newsletters, and other products and services for nonprofit organizations. This Web site also includes an online CareerBank, which can be searched by location and position type, as well as a free online newsletter.

Association of Fundraising Professionals

www.nsfre.org

> Fund raising requires a special set of skills. If you have these skills and you want to put them to good use in a career helping a nonprofit raise badly needed funds, this is the organization for you. This Web site provides information on how the association promotes charitable giving. It also shows you how you can develop your career and education as a fundraising professional.

National Council of Nonprofit Associations (NCNA)

www.ncna.org

> NCNA is a network of state and regional nonprofit associations representing more than 20,000 members in 39 states and the District of Columbia. Its mission includes raising the profile of nonprofits and providing them with the tools and leadership they need to function more effectively. Find out about current projects, locate your state association, browse job openings with member associations and partners, and find out about events in your area.

Today's Volunteer

www.ahvrp.org/ahvrp_app/index.jsp

Hospitals are a major "employer" of volunteers, and the American Society of Directors of Volunteer Services is the only national professional organization for directors of volunteer services in healthcare. At their Web site, Today's Volunteer, you can learn about ways to manage healthcare volunteers effectively, read up on news and events, find out about conferences and educational opportunities, and search for volunteer opportunities.

Glossary

ACT (American College Testing Assessment)   A standardized college admissions test measuring a student's scholastic development. Most colleges base admissions decisions on a combination of grades, activities, and scores on standardized tests such as this or the SAT.

address book   In your e-mail client software, the list of names and addresses of people to whom you frequently send messages.

affiliate program   An agreement between Web-based businesses to direct viewers to other Web sites through links, usually with a commission for resulting sales.

aggregator   Essentially any Web site that collects and filters information such as news, sports scores, job listings, or other data from other online sources and presents the combined results to the end user.

apprenticeship   A job-training program that combines classroom lessons with on-the-job training.

autoresponder   An e-mail software feature that automatically sends a response to each incoming e-mail message. For example, if a Web site instructs you to subscribe to its newsletter by sending an e-mail with "subscribe" in the subject line and you receive an immediate response, the site is using an autoresponder to manage newsletter subscriptions.

blog   Short for Web log. A Web site that serves as a publicly available personal journal.

BLS (U.S. Department of Labor Bureau of Labor Statistics)   The primary federal source of data on employment.

Boolean logic   The form of logic used by many search engines that allows you to control how narrow or broad a search you want to conduct by combining search terms in certain ways. Named for mathematician George Boole.

bot   Short for "robot." A software tool sent out by a search engine to dig through the Web for your requested information.

broadband access   A high-speed way to connect to the Internet using cable television networks or upgraded phone lines that use technologies such as Integrated Services Digital Network (ISDN) and Digital Subscriber Line (DSL). See also *dial-up access.*

browser   A program used to view Web pages. The most well-known browser program is Microsoft Internet Explorer. You also might encounter other browsers, such as Mozilla and Opera.

bulletin board   See *forum.*

career information   Descriptions of careers that might include attributes such as job requirements, skills, educational preparation, working conditions, employment outlook, and wages.

chat   To communicate online in real time. The person with whom you are chatting can see your words as you type them or immediately after you press Enter. Also called *instant messaging* or *IM.*

clearinghouse   A Web site that contains lists of other Web sites, organized by related topics.

continuing education   1. Courses available to adults who are not enrolled in a formal degree program. 2. Education undertaken after you complete a degree program to remain current in your field, sometimes required for maintaining licensure or certification. Continuing-education credits may be awarded for courses, workshops, or conferences.

contracting   Providing specific services to a company for a specified period of time and for a specified payment.

cookie   A text-only string that gets entered into a browser's memory. It allows Web sites to personalize information, help with online sales or service, or collect demographic information.

cover letter   A letter written to accompany a resume. It expresses your interest in the position you are applying for and gives an overview of your skills.

database   An organized collection of data that you can access and sort by selected criteria. For example, a job bank is an online database of available jobs. You could direct it to sort only the jobs in your state, as opposed to those across the country.

demographics   Data about the age, race, sex, income, and other details of people living in a certain area. Applications of demographic data include targeting advertising or getting an idea of the labor market in a particular area.

dial-up access   A way to connect to the Internet over standard telephone lines. Dial-up used to be found in the majority of homes, but this is no longer true.

About half of all homes have dial-up. The rest use faster broadband connections. See also *broadband access.*

Dictionary of Occupational Titles (DOT)   A reference publication, based on U.S. Department of Labor data, that classifies and briefly describes more than 12,000 jobs.

directory   A place on a computer or server where data files are stored. Directories are used to separate files into related groups and specify the location of the files on the computer.

discussion board   A Web site function that allows users to post questions or comments and respond to other people's postings. Discussion boards are commonly organized by topics or "threads."

distance learning   The ability to further your education, either toward a degree or as part of your lifelong learning, by taking courses through learning technologies other than a traditional classroom. These technologies include audiotapes, videotapes, teleconferencing, videoconferencing, and computer-based and Internet-based training.

DOL (U.S. Department of Labor)   The federal agency that oversees all federally funded labor-related programs.

domain   1. The part of your e-mail address that specifies the name of the ISP through which you access your e-mail, such as aol.com. 2. The part of a Web address that identifies the presence of a company or organization on the Internet.

download   To copy files from the Internet to your computer's hard drive.

e-lancer   A self-employed individual who contracts for work primarily through the Internet.

electronic resume   Any resume in a computerized format, usually in Microsoft Word, ASCII text, HTML, or PDF.

e-mail   Electronic mail. A written message sent from one person's online address to another's via the Internet or another computer network.

e-mail discussion list   An e-mail group in which a message posted by any member is disseminated to all members of the group, any of whom are free to respond and participate in the discussion.

emoticon   A sideways symbol in e-mail that is composed of keyboard characters. It indicates the mood of the person writing the message. For example, :) is a smiley face.

ETA (U.S. Department of Labor Employment and Training Administration)   The federal agency responsible for federally funded employment and training programs.

FAQs (Frequently Asked Questions)   A list of answers to the questions that Web site visitors are likely to ask repeatedly.

Favorites   In Internet Explorer, a way to save the addresses of your favorite Web sites so that you can return to them easily in the future.

file name   The name of the document that contains the data on a Web page. Many Web page file names end with the letters .htm or .html.

financial aid   The combination of scholarships, grants, and loans that a student uses to pay for college. Financial aid is limited to the amount of "need" that is determined for the student.

flex work   Nontraditional work arrangements such as contracting, freelancing, and temporary work.

forum   An online discussion group. Sometimes called a *bulletin board.*

franchise   A business in which you buy the right to use the name and the established procedures and products in exchange for a percentage of the profits.

free agent   A self-employed individual who works on a contract basis, often for more than one employer.

freelancer   A self-employed individual who works on a contract basis, often for more than one employer.

freeware   Software (such as games and utilities) that you can download from the Internet and use for free.

FTP (File Transfer Protocol)   A protocol for transferring files from one computer to another over the Internet.

graphical user interface (GUI)   The graphical menus, tools, and buttons you see on-screen, which help you work with a particular program using the mouse's point-and-click features.

GRE (Graduate Record Exam)   The test taken by college seniors for admission to graduate programs.

guaranty agency   The state agency or private, nonprofit organization that administers federally funded student loans.

home page   1. A Web site's initial page or starting page. 2. The page you set to appear when you first open your browser or click the Home button.

host   Any computer on a network that is a repository for services available to other computers on the network.

HTML (Hypertext Markup Language)   The coding that is used to turn regular text into a Web page that can be viewed by a browser.

hyperlink (link)   A word, phrase, or graphic on a Web page that is connected to another Internet document. By clicking it, you are taken to a related Web page, either on the same site or on a completely different Web site.

hypertext   Text that contains one or more hyperlinks.

independent professional   A self-employed individual who works on a contract basis, often for more than one employer.

indexed search engine   A search engine that locates Web pages based on text found on the page or keywords in metatags hidden in a document's coding.

infrastructure   The essential, underlying elements of an entity or organization that allow it to function.

instant messaging   See *chat*.

Internet directory   Reviews and organizes the information on the Web into categories. Each broad category, such as "Business & Economy," has more specific categories under it, and those categories have even more specific categories under them. Yahoo! is an example of an Internet directory.

Internet Explorer   Microsoft's Internet browser program, used to view and move between Web pages. Internet Explorer is built into Microsoft Windows.

Internet Service Provider (ISP)   A national or local company that, for a monthly fee, lets you connect to the Internet. Examples of national ISPs include America Online, AT&T WorldNet, and Earthlink.

internship   A program in which a student works for an employer for a specified period of time to learn about a particular occupation. The intern is sometimes paid for the work in addition to receiving college credit.

interview   To meet with a potential employer that has a job opening to determine whether you are the right person for the job. In an informational interview, you meet with a person who works in the field in which you are interested so that you can learn about the job and what you need to do to prepare for it.

job bank   A Web database of job openings. You can search for specific jobs by title, category, and geographic location, among other variables.

Job Corps   A federally funded residential education and job-training program for at-risk youth ages 16 to 24.

job fair   A meeting at which employers set up booths and speak with job seekers in an effort to recruit employees.

keyword   1. A word you type into a search engine or Web site search function to help locate information you are seeking. 2. A "hot" word (usually a noun) used in a resume. It is associated with a specific industry, profession, or job function.

labor market   The pool of both employed and unemployed persons who are currently available and willing to work; the source of applicants for a job opening.

labor market information   Data about workers, jobs, industries, and employers, generally used by program planners, analysts, administrators, researchers, employers, and job seekers.

leased employee   Someone who works for a company that sells his or her services to another company for a specified period of time. The leasing company (or temporary agency) administers the employee's salaries and benefits. See also *temp*.

link (hyperlink)   A word, phrase, or graphic on a Web page that is connected to another Internet document. By clicking it, you are taken to a related Web page, either on the same site or on a completely different Web site.

listserv™   Trademarked e-mail discussion-management software from the L-soft Corporation, often misused as a generic term for an e-mail discussion list.

load   To open a Web page with your browser. The computer temporarily copies the data from the server onto your computer's hard drive.

Macintosh (Mac)   A computer introduced by Apple Computer in 1984. The Macintosh was distinguished by its graphical user interface, which allowed users to point and click with a mouse in addition to using a keyboard to operate the system.

mailing list   A list of e-mail addresses to which you can send the same e-mail message simultaneously.

message board   A place on a Web site where people can post and respond to questions and discussion topics. See also *forum*.

metalist   A list of related Web sites posted on a Web site. Also known as a *clearinghouse*.

metasearch engine   A search engine that lets you use several search engines at a time after entering your search criteria only once.

Microsoft   The software company that introduced the Internet Explorer browser program and the Windows operating system, among other programs.

modem   The device (either inside or outside your computer) that translates information from your computer and from remote resources into a format that can travel over telephone lines.

multithreaded search engine See *metasearch engine*.

network Two or more computers or other devices connected to one another and capable of sharing data. The Internet is a massive, worldwide computer network.

networking Using your personal contacts to learn about careers and possible job openings.

newsgroup A topical online discussion group in which you can read and post messages. You can access newsgroups over the Web at http://groups.google.com.

occupational information Employment data such as wages, anticipated growth, number of people employed, number of new jobs, and other trends.

Occupational Outlook Handbook (OOH) A reference publication based on U.S. Department of Labor data. It describes the 250 most popular jobs, covering approximately 85 percent of the workforce.

O*NET The U.S. Department of Labor's electronic database of career and job information on specific occupations.

on-the-job training Job training that occurs in the workplace.

path The location of a Web page on a server. It includes the domain name, directories, and file name.

PDA (personal digital assistant) Usually includes scheduler, address book, task list, clock, and calculator software. A PDA can be synched with a desktop computer, and many can now access the Internet through Wi-Fi or other technology.

phishing An Internet scam that attempts to collect private user information to be used for identity theft. You receive an e-mail directing you to an authentic-looking Web site, where you are asked to update personal information, such as passwords and credit card, Social Security, and bank account numbers. A legitimate Web site or organization would already have these. To protect yourself from phishing, never provide personal information to a Web site based on an e-mail request.

PIN (personal identification number) A number you select or that is assigned to you for the purpose of verifying your identification for Internet transactions.

plugin A software program that works with your browser to display added information. Examples of plugins include Adobe Acrobat Reader and Macromedia Flash.

Portable Document Format (PDF or .pdf) A file format that allows documents created in any software program and saved in this format to be read through the freely downloadable Adobe Acrobat Reader software. Allows documents to appear and be printed exactly as their creator intended.

protocol   An agreed-upon format for transferring data from one computer to another.

query   To ask a database to sort and show you all the data that meets your specified criteria.

Really Simple Syndication (RSS)   A format that Web sites use to send updated headlines around the Internet. RSS allows for the automatic distribution of Internet content from news-related sites via RSS aggregators or readers, letting you receive free updates by subscribing (or clicking buttons labeled RSS or XML) to information from sites that publish content, such as news outlets or bloggers. You need an RSS reader to read a news feed.

Reserves   Military personnel who are not on active duty but who can be called into duty during a war or national crisis.

resume   An organized, written summary of your work experience, education, skills, and qualifications. Many job postings request that you submit a resume for consideration.

resume bank   A Web site where you can post a copy of your resume for potential employers to view.

robot (bot)   A software tool sent out by a search engine to dig through the Web for your requested information.

ROTC (Reserve Officer Training Corps)   A cooperative program between colleges and branches of the military that allows undergraduates to receive officer training while they attend college.

SAT (Scholastic Aptitude Test)   A standardized college admissions test. Most colleges base admissions decisions on a combination of grades, activities, and scores on standardized tests such as this or the ACT.

search engine   A Web site that lets you search for other Web sites of interest by entering a keyword or keywords in a search field. Examples of search engines include Google and Yahoo!.

self-assessment   The process of working to identify, understand, and express your skills, knowledge, abilities, interests, values, personality, motivations, passions, and anything else about you that might affect your career decisions.

server   A computer, connected to a network, that manages resources such as files or printers. Web servers contain and serve up Web page documents in response to requests from browsers.

service academy   An undergraduate college run by a branch of the armed forces that trains high school graduates to be military officers.

shareware   Software that you can download from the Internet and use for a small fee.

signature   Information that automatically appears at the bottom of every e-mail you send. It can include your name, your contact information, or your favorite quote. You can change your signature to say whatever you want.

Small Business Administration (SBA)   The federal government's primary source of small-business assistance programs under the U.S. Department of Commerce.

social networking utility   Any Web site, software, or application that lets you expand and manage a network of contacts through electronic communication, file sharing, blogging, and so on. Includes sites such as LinkedIn and Facebook.

software   A computer program that performs a specific task. Examples of software include Internet browsers, word-processing programs, spreadsheets, and games.

SOHO (small office/home office)   An acronym that reflects the growing trend of self-employed people operating small businesses from inside or outside their home environment.

teleworker (telecommuter, home worker)   An employee who works at least part-time in a home office, communicating with coworkers and clients via telephone, fax, instant messaging, and/or e-mail.

temp   A person who is employed by an agency to fill short-term positions in other companies. This person's salary and benefits are paid by the agency rather than by the companies.

TOEFL (Test of English as a Foreign Language)   Used to determine whether students are ready for mainstream classes with native speakers of English.

traffic (site traffic)   The volume of users who view a particular Web site. Increased traffic helps the owner sell advertising on the site.

upload   To send files from your computer to an Internet location.

URL (Uniform Resource Locator)   A Web site's address, such as http://www.jist.com. The first part (http://) specifies the protocol for the computers to use when transferring data; the second part specifies computer and domain name of the site you are accessing.

user name   Your unique identifier on a computer system. Many Web sites that ask you to register require you to select a user name. You use this user name and a private password to gain access again later.

Web page   A document located on another computer elsewhere on the Internet that you can view with a browser; one page within a Web site.

Web site   A group of related Web pages, compiled and sponsored by an individual or organization.

Welfare to Work   Federal welfare reform legislation intended to transition welfare recipients to the paid workforce.

Wi-Fi   Short for wireless technology network. Wi-Fi allows laptops and PDAs to connect to the Internet at high speeds without the use of wires.

Windows   Microsoft's graphical user interface and operating system for IBM-compatible PCs.

workforce   The sector of the population that is currently employed or that is ready, willing, and able to work.

workforce development   Initiatives and programs addressing the growth and maintenance of an educated, skilled workforce, coordinating with multiple employment and training service providers.

Workforce Investment Act (WIA) of 1998   Federal legislation that replaced the federal Job Training Partnership Act.

Workforce Investment Board   A policy-setting board that administers programs under the federal Workforce Investment Act, which took effect in 2000.

World Wide Web (WWW or "the Web")   A global network of information that is based on hyperlinks, which let the viewer easily jump from one Web page or Web site to a related page or site.

Index